"Suddenly they were there, lean, ghost like shapes in the moonlight with Mickey Mouse ears; wearing their dappled coats of black, tan and gold, like ink spots on blotting paper. Only a new day would reveal their full beauty. Only Man could hope to prevent their extinction."

~An extract from "Shadows in the Forest"
CD McClelland

M'vita's Struggle

Nature's Guardians Series Book 4

Written and Illustrated
by
Alisha M. Risen-Kent

Cover art by
Joycee Larsen

Dedication

For my children, Gabriel, Christopher, Syriana, and Joseph.
May you still see the splendor of our world as it is meant to be,
beautiful and untamed.

To John, my other half who has been my rock and support
through all the ups and downs.

To my parents, thank you for pushing me to be what you knew
I could be, even when the odds were stacked against me and
seemed impossible to overcome.

To my readers who have been my greatest support. Thank
you for seeing my vision and following me in this sometimes
heartbreaking journey.

Acknowledgements

I would like to give a special shout out to all those who helped
me write this book.

Thanks, Vasco Galante at Gorongosa National Park. Your
information about the park, its past and its present, was
essential for the story.

Thanks to the wonderful people of the Painted Dog Project.
You provided me with great material on wild dog behavior
behavior and vital information on their conservation status.

Thank you, most of all to National Geographic for your
priceless documentaries into the lives of African wild dogs and
other threatened species. Without your dedication to wildlife
preservation, these storied would most likely never be heard.

Translations:

Swahili:

Jata: celestial star
Kamari: moonlight
Mani: water
Musa: child
Mpendwa: beloved
Maisha: life
Nuru: light
Zuberi: strong

French:

C'est bon, un peu: It's alright, little one
un paradis: paradise
bel enfant: beautiful child

Definitions:

ensconced: hidden away

disposition: natural mental and emotional outlook or mood

despondency: state of low spirits

vehemently: showing strong emotion

camaraderie: friendship and trust between people

silhouetted: the outline of something against a lighter
background

fatigued: tired and sore, loss of energy

incapacitated: unable to move

abated: lessen, reduce

procreate: reproduce

vulnerable: at risk, in danger

ravenous: very hungry

interlopers: someone who is not where they belong

arid: harsh, lacking vegetation

regurgitate: throw up half digested food

oblivion: state of being unaware or unconscious

elusive: difficult to find

Casanova: lover boy

matriarch: a female who is the head of a family

floundering: struggle or stagger helplessly

adept: skilled or proficient st something

vigilant: watchful

undulating: move with a smooth, wave-like motion

dissension: an argument that leads to discord

melancholy: a feeling of intense sadness

resilient: able to withstand or recover quickly from difficult
situations.

permeated: spread throughout

ousted: drive out or expel someone from a position or place

uncouth: lacking good manners, refinement, or grace

The Painted Wolf

A shadow in the grass they run.
White-tufted tails flash in the sun
Their satellite ears perked high
as dawn colors paint the sky.

As one they move with grace.
Their feet quiet as they race.
Their prey stands unawares
as the pack a pounce prepares

When morning turns to day
with full bellies the pack does lay
sleeping off the African heat
to nature songs so sweet.

Altogether they stand as one
barking and yipping with everyone
the pack takes a moment to bond and play
before once again joining life's fray.

~Gabriel Kent

Table of Contents:

Chapter One: Family

The world I was born into can only be described as saturated with energy. It was early spring in Africa, a time of rebirth and warmth. The seasonal rains had passed and the world was bright and green. Even before I could see or hear, I could smell the land growing around me. It wasn't long before my blurry eyes opened to a world that would become my own.

I had ten siblings that Mother and the rest of the pack doted over. Our pack was large. So large, in fact, I lost count of how many individuals actually lived among us. And every one of them emitted their own energy. I can't ever remember a quiet moment in those early days, except for when the pack slept.

In my first weeks, when my legs refused to work properly, Mother kept us ensconced in her den, hidden from the countless predators prowling through the grasses. It wasn't long, however, that we outgrew our tiny home and began to venture outside into the warm daylight. I loved these excursions the most. The beauty of the world around me tempted me too much to stay hidden.

The best thing about having such a large family is the limitless food. It seemed like every member had a morsel to share with us after a hunt. Our bellies were always full and we were surrounded by boundless love and affection. Oh yeah, and we always had a babysitter when the rest of the pack left to hunt. Sometimes, the guardian was not much older than us.

One particular afternoon, a few weeks after we began venturing out of the den, my oldest brother had the bright idea of slipping past the young guardian. She faced away from us and lay still so long we believed she slept. Still, I had a tiny thread of doubt eating away at me.

"Sasha," I whispered in my brother's over-large ear. "I don't think this is a good idea."

His satellite ear flicked back, smacking me in the nose. "It's fine, M'vita. She'll never know we're gone."

Despite my better judgement, I followed Sasha and my other nine siblings from the shelter of the den. We had just made it to the edge of the clearing when we felt a warm breeze against our necks. As one, we turned to the irate face of our guardian.

Standing tall above us, she smiled mischievously and cocked her head. "Now, where could you little demons be slipping off to?" she asked with mock sweetness.

"Just getting some fresh air," Sasha answered, his shoulders hunched under the weight of her stare.

Her smile disappeared and she pulled back her lips, flashing her canines. It was all the warning we needed. We ran back to the den, our white-tufted tails tucked between our legs!

The next couple of weeks followed the same routine. Every day Sasha would get a bit bolder and we would sneak further and further out from the den until one day, we had made it all the way into the grass. Our babysitter that day was an elderly female who had lost nearly all of her fur. She lay panting in the shade of a tree near the den. Her eyes were closed but her ears flicked relentlessly at the flies biting them. A nearby herd of buffalo snorted at one another, masking the tiny sounds we made as we slipped past our sleeping sentinel.

That was one thing we had mastered over the weeks: moving silently. Our legs had grown faster than the rest of us, allowing us to walk on our toes to keep from making noise. We had taken on the characteristic bounce in our step shared by the adults. I always enjoyed watching Mother and the others run around. To me, it looked like an intricate dance that I was desperate to learn.

The old female barely stirred as eleven quickly growing pups slipped past her and into the thick brush.

We moved in the direction opposite the buffalo. It was a risk, as that meant we had less outside noise to cover our own but none of us really wanted to get any closer to the behemoths just outside our den.

It had taken the old female a while to fall asleep and in the back of my mind, I worried that the pack would be returning soon. Not only would we get in trouble for being out of the den, again, if we moved too far, we might miss lunch. My stomach growled at the thought and Sasha snapped his head in my direction.

"Sorry!" I whispered and lowered my head.

He turned back toward the front and continued leading us down a path he chose at random. In hindsight, I wondered why we always followed him, even though we knew we were going to get in trouble. We always got caught and although I suspect Mother knew it was Sasha leading the charge, we never said it out loud.

Our journey out of the den on this day would forever change our lives, even though we didn't know it at the time. We were gone for quite some time before we heard the pack approaching. In fact, Sasha had managed to get us lost in the tall grasses. The rains had left everything vibrant and green, to include the grass we were currently lost in. Following the sound of two dozen barking dogs, we managed to make it back to the den.

Mother and the other adults waited for us at the entrance. We fell on them, whining and licking their mouths so they would regurgitate our lunch. It was eaten nearly before it hit the ground. Our sharp baby teeth made short work of the meal. As we were finishing up, Mother called us to attention.

"I noticed you were all gone when we returned from the hunt," she said, casually. "Tahi says you left nearly an hour ago."

We all looked at each other. So, the old female wasn't asleep as we had thought. Mother seemed to understand that look and even though none of us spoke a word, she answered our silent conversation.

"Tahi is too old to chase after younglings," Mother continued. "She figured if you were old enough to brave the buffalo, you could handle yourselves. However, you must understand the danger you put yourselves in every time you wander from the safety of the den. What would have happened if a predator came too close? You wouldn't have time to reach the burrow and Tahi cannot protect all of you from a predator if it wishes to get you."

We all dropped our heads. Sasha even laid on his belly. We hadn't thought about that possibility. Our actions could have put even Tahi in danger. Mother sighed and lowered her head to our level.

"Next time, do not wander so far away."

"Yes, Mother," we all cried in unison.

With the moment passed, the rest of the pack surrounded us, finding any place they could to stretch out and rest. From the corner of my eye I noticed Tahi, belly full and lounging against a rock. I turned to her and smiled. With a wink she let me know that all was forgiven.

When the sun set that night, my siblings and I crawled back into the den. The night brought predators that kept even the adults on high alert. It was not uncommon for lions or leopards to slip in while we slept and reek havoc on the pack. I once heard a tale of a leopard making off with an adult male. The pack could do nothing to stop the hungry feline.

As we settled down to sleep, Sasha turned to me, his energy still overflowing. I always wondered how he could still have so much after our adventures but the pup never seemed to tire. Of course, when he did finally run out, he slept like the dead.

"M'vita," he whispered, not wanting to attract Mother who slept just outside the den.

"Go to sleep, Sasha," I grumbled. "Aren't you even a little tired?"

"Yeah, right! Do you really think it is that dangerous out there?" He scooted on his belly a little more toward me.

"Yes, I do. Mother doesn't just say things to scare us." I tucked my nose between my feet hoping he would get the message.

"But...we were out there all day and didn't see anything."

Kanji, the second born after Sasha, lifted his head at Sasha's statement. "Maybe that's a good thing," he said. "Then again, if there *were* something out there, and it had eaten you, we would have less trouble on our hands."

"Shut it, Kanji!" Sasha snapped. "No one said you had to come."

"Guys, let's not fight," said Suri, my younger sister. She was always playing peacemaker and had a gentle disposition. She also had a way of dissolving fights before they ever really started.

Sasha and Kanji glared at each other for another minute before dropping their heads and closing their eyes. Sighs from our other siblings showed that the short confrontation had kept them awake as well. As usual, I had a small twinge in my belly for my forlorn brother.

Sucking down my own sigh, I tried to reassure him. "Sasha, in time, we will be able to join the pack and experience all that they do. For now, let's just be pups, secure in the knowledge that we are safe and protected with full bellies and a warm place to sleep." I slipped closer to him and bumped him with my shoulder.

He cracked a smile and bumped me back, much harder than I had bumped him, causing me to fall on Horu, another brother. Horu yelped, having been awoken and turned to snap at me. So much for trying to ease tensions! In reflex, I snapped back causing him to fall into even more siblings. What followed was an all out rumble where puppies, who should have been sleeping, were instead growling and barking.

A sharp reprimand from the den entrance had our heads snapping in the direction. Mother stood there staring down at us. Her glare was all we needed. We quickly huddled up together and closed our eyes. As soon as Mother left, Sasha chuckled.

"Well, I feel better," he smirked.

That little…! I thought to myself. The brat planned it all along. Suppressing another sigh, I put it behind me and finally drifted off to sleep.

Chapter Two: Danger

The following week we stayed close by the den, Mother's warning fresh in our minds. Although Sasha ached to venture further, he knew we would no longer follow him. Instead, he used his pent up energy to bully the rest of us. He would often plow into one of us, causing the offended to fight back. More often than not, this was either me or Kanji, as we seemed to have nearly as much energy as him.

Our babysitter of the day, usually one of the younger adults from the pack, would watch with patient resignation. If we became too loud, he or she would snap at us and tell us to keep it down. While I appreciated the break from Sasha, I could never figure out why we had to be quite. It was daylight, the pack was off hunting, and we weren't supposed to be sleeping. In fact, when the pack returned, which usually wasn't much longer after they left, the whole clearing was filled with noise. We would soon learn the answer to that question.

Not long after the morning hunt, the pack lay lounging around the den digesting their breakfast. It was a quiet morning, more so than usual. The heat of the day already soaked through our fur, despite the early hour and the shade around the den. The heat, mixed with full bellies meant that my siblings and I slept soundly. The rest of the pack slept as they usually did, lightly and on alert.

On this day, however, the pack was not as alert as usual. Perhaps it was the heat or maybe their prey was larger than normal, their over-full bellies making them too tired to stay fully alert. Whatever the reason, no one saw the danger until it was too late.

Nani, one of the older males, slept near the outer edge of the clearing underneath a scrub bush. Although his ear flicked back and forth, I suspect it was more to keep the flies at bay than to listen for danger. Before the pack realized what happened, something large jumped from the tall grass, grabbed him, and disappeared. The only way we even knew something had happened was because Nani let out a single yelp before being dragged away.

The pack jumped to their feet, many plunging into the grass to try and rescue our pack member. Mother signaled for us to run for cover and we dashed to the den. Below, we could here the pack barking and growling at something and the responding snarls from some big cat. Nani never came back and once it was safe for us to leave the den, I noticed the sadness in the pack's faces.

That night, Mother moved the den. She said it was no longer safe. I suspect it also held sad memories from losing Nani. One by one, she moved us. The trip was long and arduous. She carried us in her mouth the whole way, stopping occasionally to readjust her grip or to take a quick break. Working through the night, she risked predators finding her or us. Half the pack stayed at the old den while the other half stayed at the new one, making sure we were safe.

Unlike other times when the pack was awake and moving, that night everyone was deadly quiet. I had never heard the pack so silent before. Even my siblings and I kept quiet. By morning, Mother was exhausted. We cuddled next to her while the rest of the pack went to hunt.

"Mother," Kanji asked quietly, not wanting to wake her if she slept. When she raised her head, he continued. "What was it that took Nani? He was so big and strong."

Mother rolled onto her side and licked Kanji under the chin. I think it was for her own comfort as much as it was for his.

"Nani was taken by a leopard, little one," she answered, sadness seeping into her voice. "They are bigger than us and they are stealthy. They also usually hunt at night. He attacked us because he hasn't been eating well."

"Is Nani ever coming back?" I could tell Kanji was close to tears.

"No, youngling. He is not. He has joined a much greater pack that watches over us all. Do not worry about him any longer."

Kanji snuggled closer to Mother and closed his eyes.

The morning after moving to the new den I realized that something was wrong with some of my siblings. Three of them did not run to the pack when they returned with food. After eating my fill, I turned to see them cuddled together near the den entrance.

I called to them, thinking maybe they were just sleeping too soundly, despite the loud raucous the pack was making. When they did not move, I went to them.

Jata, Kamari, and Maji lay panting on their sides. While they *were* awake, they did not move at my approach. I bumped my head against theirs and pulled on their ears. Still, they did not respond. I turned toward Mother and whined to get her attention. She looked my way but did not approach. Even the other pack members seemed distracted.

Sasha, Kanji, and Suri did notice and came to see why I was distressed. When they noticed our two brothers and sister, they tried to rouse them as I had done, with the same results.

"Come on, Kamari," Sasha said, biting him on his scruff. "Stop lazing around or you're going to be really hungry later."

"I'm sorry, Sasha," Kamari all but whispered. "I don't feel so well. I'll eat something later."

Jata and Maji grunted in agreement. Satisfied that they were at least aware of their surroundings, the rest of my siblings and I laid down next to them and fell to sleep.

When we woke some time later, I didn't notice at first that there were fewer pups than usual. The rest of the pack was already awake and were jumping around and playing. Wanting to be part of the excitement, I ran over and began nipping at the larger adults. So lost in my blissfully innocent fun, I did not stop to think about my sick siblings. Later, when I was much older, I would understand that the adults were trying to distract me from the tragedy that had unfolded.

Once the pack had been reenergized, they set off to hunt. Mother, in an uncharacteristic show of affection, allowed us to nurse from her, something we hadn't done since being weened several days prior. Once we were done, we engaged in our own form of play which was very much like the one the older dogs had done. When the pack returned that evening, we gorged ourselves on meat. Soon after, we slipped into the den and fell asleep. It wasn't until the next morning that I realized Jata, Kamari, and Maji were no longer with us.

The days that followed were bittersweet. On the one hand, we missed our siblings. Mother said the journey had been too hard on them and their tiny bodies had simply given out. When I asked why the rest of us were okay, she said that some of us were just stronger than others. She said Jata, Kamari, and Maji had left to join Nani in his new pack. He would watch over them now.

Despite our sadness, or maybe because of it, the rest of the pack paid us extra attention, allowing us to wrestle extra hard without giving a sharp reprimand. Sasha, of course, found this especially pleasing. He would roughhouse with the bigger males to his heart's content. Watching him, I knew he would be a great hunter someday, maybe even an alpha.

Of all of us, I think Suri took our siblings loss the hardest. It took days for her to come out of her despondency. While she would eat and sleep with the rest of us, she would not join in on the playing. As the most docile of my siblings, she was closest to those who left. In time, however, she pulled through and returned to us.

The new den sat beneath a large acacia tree, its wide branches curving out over most of the clearing. It provided shelter for the entire pack and since the clearing around the den was lower than the surrounding grasses, it kept the pack hidden from predators.

Two more weeks passed as we fell into our normal routine. Sasha, ever the adventurer, wanted to explore beyond the clearing as we had done at the old den. However, after the many losses we had already experienced in our young lives, we were vehemently opposed to the idea. Kanji was especially emotional.

"Sasha, you're an idiot!" he said to our oldest brother. "Don't you get how dangerous it is?"

"Calm down, Kanji!" Sasha defended. "I wasn't going to go very far. Just up to the top of the rise. I want to see what it looks like up there."

Kanji jumped on Sasha, throwing him to the ground. We all stared in fascination. Sasha was the biggest and strongest of us and Kanji, despite being second largest and almost as energetic as Sasha, was more like Suri. He didn't like confrontation but something about Sasha made him lose his cool. The fact that he had just slammed his brother to the ground showed just how far Sasha had pushed him.

"Kanji," I said calmly to my fuming brother. "Sasha was only jesting. He would never do something so stupid." I threw Sasha a pointed glare, daring him to dispute me. Luckily, he just chuckled and rolled onto his feet.

"Yeah, Kanji," he said. "I was only kidding. You shouldn't be so serious all the time."

"The next time you have the idea to do something stupid, even as a joke, keep it to yourself. We've lost enough pack members to worry about the stupidity of another." Kanji turned his back on Sasha and stormed off toward the den.

I looked from Sasha to Kanji while the rest of our siblings moved off toward Mohaji, our babysitter for the day. Sasha turned back to the path that led up to the rise. I knew what he was thinking. I just hoped he was smart enough not act on those thoughts. Kanji sat by himself, looking up into the leaves of the acacia tree. Leaving Sasha to his thoughts, I approached Kanji.

"He can't help it, you know. He has the makings of an alpha," I said.

"I know. But if he rushes it, he's going to get himself killed. And then what kind of alpha will he be?"

"True. He just has some growing up to do. I think, deep down, he knows what he's supposed to do. When it comes down to it, I don't think he is going to do anything that is going to get himself or anyone else hurt."

Kanji looked at me and smiled. He sat there for several minutes just smiling at me. Finally, I smiled back.

"What?" I asked.

"You have the makings of an alpha, too," he answered.

I didn't mean to laugh but what was I supposed to do? The idea of me being an alpha was just too funny not to laugh.

"What gave you that idea?" I asked, still chuckling.

"Look at you. Most of us follow you out of the den when the sun comes up. When its playtime, we take our cues from you. When there is a fight, you are right there to dispel it. And you may not notice it, but Sasha listens to you more than anyone else, like he is seeking your approval. Sure, Suri is our peacekeeper, but if we had a leader, it would be you."

I sat there and absorbed all that he had said. How could I have missed all that? I saw myself as a kind of down-the-middle personality, neither leader material nor follower. To have Kanji, one of the strongest of my siblings both physically and mentally, tell me that they all look to me for guidance was a shock to my system.

"Thanks, Kanji," I said. "I'll do my best to continue being the dog you think I am."

Kanji chuckled. "You don't have to try, M'vita. It's in your blood." He leaned his shoulder against mine and closed his eyes.

Chapter Three: Growing Up

We grew quickly over the following several weeks.
Our fur changed from black to the splotchy whites
and yellows of the adults. Our legs grew longer, also
sporting the patchwork that covered our new fur. The
white tufts on our tails, something that hadn't
changed as we got bigger, now had longer fur that
whipped through the air as we greeted the pack

everyday. The biggest change was probably our ears that were nearly as big as our heads. We were becoming miniature versions of the adults.

Sasha and Kanji had settled their differences and were back to being playful brothers. In fact, they seemed like they were closer than before. Suri even changed somewhat as we got older. She was still the peacekeeper but she also became more outgoing as she grew into the dog she would become. I liked seeing her have a more active role in the pack.

Horu, Zani, Matika, and Zephyr continued as they were. Horu always ended up the brunt of all Sasha's antics. I think Sasha did this because Horu responded so extremely. The little male would lash out at our older brother only to end up on his back. Zani, the last of our brothers kept quiet, like Suri. He liked to attack when it was least expected. Watching him, I thought he would make a great scout one day. He could move quiet as a leopard.

Matika was much like Maji had been. They were the closest of my siblings and I think she took it hardest when Maji died. As we grew older, however, she began to come into her own. She spent much of her time with the adults, learning things that would benefit her when she became an adult herself. Lastly was Zephyr. As the smallest and youngest of all of us, Zephyr fought tooth and nail for everything she got. She was a fierce little fighter and I knew one day, she would be an asset to the pack.

At five months old, the den felt cramped and too small to hold us. Still, it was the safest place for us to sleep at night. Mother no longer slept at the entrance. After we retired, she disappeared somewhere among the rest of the pack. I wanted to sneak to the entrance once just so I could see where she went but the curious stares of my siblings had me laying back down. The last thing I needed was to set a bad example for those who looked to me for guidance.

Kanji and Sasha whispered among themselves and for the briefest of moments, I felt all alone. I missed the camaraderie I once shared with my brothers. Even then, I was glad that Kanji and Sasha were no longer fighting. As I dropped my chin to my feet, I heard Kanji call to me. Glancing quickly at my other siblings, I noticed they were all engaged in their own conversations: Horu, Zephyr and Matika in one conversation and Suri and Zani in another. I quietly gathered my feet and approached my brothers.

"So, we were thinking of asking Mother if we could leave the den tomorrow," Kanji whispered.

"We aren't asking to leave the clearing, just the den," Sasha explained, probably seeing the look of doubt on my face. "What do you think?"

"Well, it is pretty crowded in here," I conceded. "She might let us as long as we stay near the entrance, just in case."

"Will you go with us to ask her?" Sasha asked. Kanji nodded his head in agreement. "She listens to you."

I sighed. So that was why they called me over. "Sure, I'll be the messenger."

"Thanks, M'vita!" they both said in unison.

I chuckled at their enthusiasm. With that important matter out of the way, they snuggled up to me, one on each side. I chuckled again and laid my head across Kanji's back. Stretching out my long legs, I laid them across Sasha's back. *Awww! There's nothing like a soft fur bed!*

Sometime during the night we were wakened by a noise that reverberated through the walls of the den. Our heads jumped up trying to find the source of the sound but it was not coming from underground. I reassured my siblings, telling them to stay put while I carefully made my way to the entrance. Mother laid next to the opening, looking off into the distance. She did not seem alarmed, only alert. I took that as a good sign.

"Mother," I called softly, not wanting to wake the rest of the pack. She looked at me briefly before turning back to the sound, which seemed to come from every direction at once. "What is that noise?"

"It is a lion," she answered. "He is telling other predators that this is his land."

I could not understand her calmness. "Are you not afraid?" I asked.

"He is far away. Lion roars travel several miles. As long as we are quiet, we are safe here. Go back into the den. Lions are too big to fit in there so it is the safest place for you to be."

"Yes, Mother." With one last look around, I shivered and slipped back into the den. My siblings all looked at me expectantly. "We will not be leaving the den any time soon," I said as way of answering them. Kanji and Sasha slouched with disappointment and I think a little bit of relief. None of us wanted to be out there at that moment.

The next day, the pack acted like nothing was out of the ordinary. We rose with the sun and greeted each other with enthusiasm. The adults swarmed us, covering us with kisses and affection before setting off for the hunt. Some of my siblings tried to engage the babysitter in a game of chase. He was a young male and although he tried to stay alert, the pups proved to be too much of a distraction. I found myself pulled into the game as well.

Too much time passed after the pack left and I began to worry that something had happened. Finally, they came over the ridge and fell into the clearing. As usual, we flocked them, begging for meat to fill our bellies. However, none of the pack members had meat to give. The hunt had been unsuccessful. Our stomachs grumbled at their empty state but try as we might, we would not be eating that morning.

Concerned, I asked Mother why there was no food.

"When we are hunting, we sometimes have to decide if the risk of bringing down prey is worth the pack's safety," she began. "Today, while running down an antelope, we passed a pride of lions. They were some ways off but had we succeeded in bringing the antelope down, the lions could have ambushed us before we finished feeding, leading to injury or death to many of the pack. Knowing that, we called off the chase for now. We will try again this evening."

I admired Mother most at that point. To be able to make a split-second decision that would impact the pack in the heat of the moment is the trait of a true leader. There was a reason Mother was the alpha of our pack.

The rest of the day we slept, nursing our empty bellies. Without food, we did not have the energy to play. I think the adults were actually happy about this. It allowed them some much needed rest, especially after the restless night. That evening, they once again left to hunt. This time, they were successful and came back with full bellies. We ate well and then, after a round of roughhousing, we lounged around with the rest of the pack. As the sun began to set, we retreated back into the den.

The next several nights were filled with the roars of lions. We had become so accustomed to the sound that we began to sleep through it. The sounds never came closer so Mother did not move the den. I was grateful for this, worried that doing so would result in more losses. Kanji and Sasha never brought up leaving the den again, despite the relative safety that Mother felt. I think they preferred the cramped confines to the roars above ground.

A week or so after the roars began, the pack had begun moving farther from the den to hunt. I gathered this was for two reasons: one, prey moved farther away as the best grass was eaten and two, to keep the lions far from the den. This meant the pack was gone for longer stretches of time. I could see the apprehension in our babysitter's face every time something made a noise nearby. Sohi would chirp, causing us to dash for the den at every false alarm.

She also made us play quietly, something that was nearly impossible for eight five-month old puppies. Still, I urged my brothers and sisters to try and not make things harder for Sohi. As it was, she seemed on the verge of a panic attack. Before the pack came back with the morning meal, we realized her panic was well founded.

We were tumbling around near the edge of the clearing, making more noise than we should have. Sasha chomped down on Horu's foot and the younger brother responded exactly how Sasha wanted. Horu yelped loudly and lashed out at Sasha, growling and snapping. This caused an all out battle between Horu, Sasha, Kanji, and Zephyr. I sat back laughing at their antics and getting ready to tell them to quiet down. I was not fast enough.

Sohi jumped to her feet and barked as a young male lion leapt over the grass into the clearing. We dashed for the den but we were too far away and there were too many of us to fit all at once. Sohi charged the lion, hoping to distract it while we ran to safety. I heard her yelp as the lion swiped at her. Before she could get back to her feet, the lion was upon us.

Matika, Suri, Horu, and Kanji had already made it safely into the den. That left me, Sasha, Zephyr, Zani, and the injured Sohi to face the beast between us and safety. Sasha and Zephyr came at the lion's flanks on either side, causing it to whip its head back and forth to reach them. Me and Sohi faced him head on, attempting to get him to move enough for the others to make a dash for the entrance. Zani stood paralyzed with fear, too far from the den to make it, even if we could make an opening.

The lion sat on his haunches, protecting it from the sharp teeth of my siblings. He roared in anger and frustration, probably not expecting so much resistance. Sohi lashed out and grabbed him by his adolescent mane, managing to pull him away from the entrance. Sasha and Zephyr took the opportunity to run into the den. I had a clear shot as well but Zani still stood paralyzed. I wanted to go to him but the pleading look in Sohi's eyes had me dashing for safety as well.

From the protection of the den we heard Zani yelp, followed by barking and growling from Sohi. A moment later it was all over. The lion dug at the entrance, trying to get to us. We huddled as far back as we could get. Finally, the most beautiful sound reached our ears: the barking of the pack. The lion, not wanting to take on the entire pack, turned tail and ran. Mother slipped into the den and we crowded around her, whimpering and shaking.

"It's alright now," she reassured. "You're safe now."

"Mother! Zani and Sohi were still out there!" I cried.

"They have gone with the others, little one," she said, her voice shaking with emotion. "We do not need to worry for them anymore."

My chest was heavy with grief. How could Mother be so calm at a time like this? Would I ever be as strong as she?

Chapter Four: Running With the Pack

Mother made a decision the next day that would forever change our lives. We would be moving again. Only this time, we would not be moving to another den. We would be following the pack as they traveled across Mother's land. She said it was safer to keep moving. Den sites attract predators. By moving, we were less likely to be spotted.

I could feel the energy seep into me from my siblings excitement, despite our recent losses. It was a right of passage, a sign that we were no longer pups but a part of the pack. My chest swelled with my own excitement. I couldn't wait to see what this new world had to offer.

The next morning, the pack gathered near the den for the last time. The sun struggled against the horizon, painting the sky a deep red orange. Everything was silhouetted against a fiery backdrop. Heat waves already sizzled against the earth, making the ground look like an endless lake.

We sat as one looking off into the distance at our world. A world that looked brand new to me and my brothers and sisters. In fact, I think that was the first time we watched a sunrise as a pack and I can't ever remember anything, either before or after, being as beautiful as that moment. It only lasted a few minutes as the sun finally breached the horizon and jumped into the sky, taking its golden splendor with it.

That was the last time any of us ever saw our den again.

Despite our many adventures outside of our childhood home, nothing could have prepared us for the endless running and moving across the rough and uneven African terrain. By mid-day, our feet were sore and tired, the once soft pads broken and bleeding. Mother, understanding our need for a break, stopped the pack near a stream to rest. After quenching our thirst, we soaked our paws in the cool water. I turned to Sasha who looked both excited and exhausted.

"Well, brother," I said. "How do you like our grand adventure now?"

"This is so much better than being cooped up in that den," he answered. I could tell by the contented look on his face that he meant it.

Mother approached us soon after that. It always amazed me how she never seemed winded, even after all the running we had done. While we lounged around trying to catch our breaths, she stood tall and regal, the alpha of the pack. We all looked up at her, our large ears swiveled in her direction.

"You have all done well today," she said. "You will get stronger as you get older and your feet will harden so they no longer tear. After you are rested, we are going to hunt. Do you think you can keep up?"

"Yes, Mother!" we all said in unison.

She nodded and turned back to the rest of the pack. She nudged a few that she passed in an affection manner. I watched her in fascination. We never knew which of the many males of the pack was our father and it had become a game to us to speculate which one had won Mother's affection. As I watched her pass by each member and rub against them, I once again wondered who it could be.

Too soon, the pack found their feet again and began to set out. With a deep sigh I, too, rose to my feet and followed my siblings out into the grass. In preparation for the hunt, the pack had a play session to excite their muscles. As a young pup, I didn't really understand the need for this. However, after my first hunt, I realized how important it was to build adrenaline before undertaking a long run. The pack barked and jumped around each other, nipping tails and ears until the energy around us became palpable. Then, as one we turned and began our hunt.

Not long after heading out, we heard the shuffling of a heard of gazelle. They were not far away but the grass obscured my view of them. Luckily, it also obscured their view of us. When we were just outside their line of view, Mother charged the herd. The rest of the pack moved around the herd to outflank them. This created a bottleneck effect that allowed Mother to isolate an injured buck. The rest of the herd pulled away, leaving the buck to fight the pack alone.

Despite the fact that gazelle are fast and fleet, we, as wild dogs, are uniquely designed to hunt them. Our legs are long and slender and when we run, we land on our toes, much like a cat. This means we spend very little time actually on the ground. Our bodies are also streamlined to cut through the air. Lastly, as top hunters and runners, we store extra oxygen in the muscles of our back legs. When we break into an extensive run, these muscles release the oxygen into our bloodstream, keeping us from experiencing muscle fatigue that could mean the failure of a hunt.

It would normally take the pack several minutes to wear down a gazelle enough to fall it. However, the buck we chased had an injured hoof and when he placed it down at a wrong angle, it no longer held his weight. The pack fell on him in a frenzy. As my brothers and I reached the gazelle, they parted to allow us to eat our fill first. My grumbling stomach welcomed the meal and within minutes, we were full and sated.

Once we were done, the others moved in. There was no growling or fighting. The meal did not last long. Once everyone was fed, the only thing left was the skin and bones of the gazelle. I noticed movement from behind the kill and perked my ears in that direction. A dog-like creature with a sloped back and spots was slowly approaching the carcass. For every two steps it took forward, it took one back, cautious of the large pack near the kill. It was easily twice as big as our largest male but it cowered as it came closer.

Mother was suddenly on her feet and heading toward us. She didn't seemed frightened, only cautious as she beckoned us to rise. The rest of the pack seemed to notice the interloper as well and moved to surround us, barking and snapping at the animal. With nothing left to leave us there, we turned and disappeared into the grass. I ran to catch up with Mother who was moving at a leisurely pace.

"Mother," I called. She turned her head to me without slowing her stride. "What creature was that?"

"That was a hyena," she answered. "Alone, it is no match for a pack our size. However, if there is a pack of them, they can cause serious injury or death to our kind. If you ever see one when you are alone, run the other way. They can be very dangerous."

"Yes, Mother."

"You and your siblings did well today," she continued. "You will all be great hunters one day. Maybe you will even be alpha of your own pack."

"My own pack?"

"Yes, M'vita. When you are older, you will leave here in search of your own pack. If you are strong and courageous, you will one day be an alpha like me."

"Why would I ever want to leave? This is my family. I could never imagine leaving everyone." The very thought of leaving everything and everyone I'd ever known scared me more than anything else. I thought about all the energy I felt within the pack. Why would anyone ever want to leave that behind?

"Worry not, youngling," Mother continued, turning her head back to the front. "That is still some time away, after you have grown up and experienced a bit of life. When the time comes, you will be ready."

That night, once the pack was settled and resting, my siblings and I cuddled next to Mother. It was the first time we had done so in days and was a memory that I would cherish for the rest of my life. Sasha, still filled with the excitement of the day, chatted on about everything that had happened. Mother chuckled at his childish view of the world but indulged him anyway. I simply soaked in the pack's energy, as I had done from the first time I felt it. The pack was content with full bellies. Just as we had watched the sun rise that morning, we sat together and watched it set.

As I was laying my head down on my paws, just about to close my eyes, an older male approached Mother. I realized it was Kion, the alpha male and the largest and strongest member of the pack. Typically he stayed near the outer fringes of the pack, keeping a wary eye out for danger. It surprised me that he approach Mother now, especially given the easy grace and familiarity he used while approaching her. Mother's face softened as she noticed him and licked him beneath his chin.

I moved my eyes around the clearing without lifting my head. All my siblings were asleep. Sasha snored lightly, his tongue lolling out of his mouth. A sudden movement had my eyes turning back to Mother. Kion had settled next to her and spoke softly against her ear. While I could not hear what he was saying, I suddenly realized who he was. Kion was our father. It all made since given that they were the two alphas of the pack. A smile stretched across my face at the realization. I decided at that moment that I would keep the secret to myself. Let my siblings continue to speculate. Soaking in the energies of my parents, I closed my eyes and drifted off to sleep, the smile still on my face.

Chapter Five: Reunion

The rest of summer flew by quickly as the vibrant green grasses of the rainy season began to die off and turn brown and brittle. This was a time of plenty for us. Herds became weak and needed to move constantly in search of fresh grass and water. The rivers and lakes that snaked through the terrain began to dry out, forcing grazers and predators into close proximity of each other. I would soon learn that the grazers were not the only ones at risk near these watering holes.

A few weeks after leaving the den, we all lounged in the shade after a big meal. Every few minutes, one of the adults would raise their head, look around, and then lay back down again. I found this curious until I realized what they were doing. They were keeping an eye out for danger. It seemed exhausting to me, who just wanted to sleep the day away. In fact, my siblings were doing just that. However, every time a head popped up, it grabbed my attention and I lifted mine as well, trying to determine what they were looking at. My experiences of late had taught me to always be on my guard.

Around late afternoon, just as I was finally dozing off, one of the older males suddenly jumped to his feet, his ears pulled back and a low growl emanating from his throat. I snapped my head in his direction as the other adults also found their feet. Their posture was confusing as some were on the defensive while others were openly curious. Then I smelled it, the scent of a dog not from our pack. Or so I assumed at the time.

From the thick brush came bounding three young males with ears pulled back and heads lowered. Their tails whipped back and forth like white flags of surrender and a soft, high-pitch whimper-bark echoed the clearing. Mother and the other adults and yearlings responded in kind, licking and nuzzling the young males as though welcoming back a wayward son, which I soon realized was exactly what they were doing.

The three young males were from a litter Mother had two seasons prior. Not long before my siblings and I had been born, they had left the pack in order to create one of their own. But living out on your own is tough and it seemed the males had found it too hard and returned home. The pack welcomed them back as though they had never left.

The commotion woke my siblings and we ran to be part of the activity. The males greeted us the same as the rest of the pack. The added energy from the new arrivals filled me with excitement. After the initial greetings, Mother signaled for the pack to move. With three more mouths to feed, we headed off to find the herds.

The harsh African summer bore down on everyone equally. By now, the green grasses were nearly completely gone. A few hardy bushes retained their green leaves but these were covered in long spines that discouraged the grazers from picking from them. The water holes shrank to muddy bogs full of overheated and irritable crocodiles. Only the bravest of grazers approached them.

Since we no longer had a den to return to, the pack was constantly moving. Every evening found us some place new. At the time, I thought Mother moved the pack from place to place without rhyme or reason. However, as I matured, I realized she simply moved along the boundaries of her territory, each dog making their mark to discourage other dogs from entering our borders.

One particular afternoon, when my siblings and I were around six months old, I had my first encounter with dogs not from our pack. The memory is one that will stay with me the rest of my life.

We were lounging near the far border of our territory, butting up against the no-man's land between packs. The herds had been moving, looking for a fresh source of water and had crossed over into this land. For the moment, we stayed in our territory. Having just fed that morning, we did not need to follow them and Mother knew they would eventually wander back our way.

Eventually came sooner rather than later. The ground rumbled beneath us, sending up small dust clouds around our resting bodies. We jumped to our feet looking for the source and watched as the herd stampeded back toward us. Mother scanned the area, looking for the hunter that had spooked the herd. If it were a lion, we would need to move.

Instead of lions, a rival pack chased the herd back onto our land. However, instead of stopping at the border as we had done, they followed them into our territory. The pack reacted immediately, charging the pack just as they breached the border.

The rival pack stopped when they noticed us and the herd disappeared through the trees. Mother and Father took point and growled at the rivals, sending them a stern warning to leave. The rival pack was much smaller and thinner and I suspected they desperately needed a meal. But Mother would not back down.

Perhaps it was hunger or inexperience but the rival pack did not back down either. Taking Mother's challenge, they charged the pack. Tahi immediately pulled me and my siblings back, creating a protective barrier between us and the rival pack.

"Let us through, Mia," the alpha male said to Mother. "We need this meal."

"You are on our territory, Shion," Mother answered, her head lowered in warning. "You know you cannot come here."

"We are starving. If we do not eat soon, we will die. As your brother, let me pass this once."

"I have my own pack to feed. I cannot let you wander my lands."

"We do not have a choice! The two-legs have chased us from our home. Already my pack is half what it once was."

Mother seemed saddened for a moment but she held her ground. The rest of the pack lined up around her, offering her support should she need it.

"You always were stubborn and hard-headed," Shion snarled. "So be it."

With his final words, he launched at her, followed by the rest of his pack. Our pack answered in kind and an all-out battle ensued. The packs tumbled together on the dry ground creating a cloud I could barely see through. The dogs from both packs snarled and snapped. Occasionally, one would yelp and jump back.

While I was confident Mother would win the fight, I still worried about injuries. An injury during a fight could mean the death of a dog. In a matter of minutes, the fight was over. The rival pack limped off back to their territory. Mother took inventory of our own pack.

Three dogs were injured in the fight, one of them seriously. Musa, one of the young males that had just returned, had a deep wound on his hip. He limped over to where we rested and fell onto his uninjured side. The other two dogs had injuries to their legs and neck. None of them would be able to hunt until they healed.

Chapter Six: Life Lessons

That night, we gathered around Musa. Mother seemed to understand how serious his wound was and what the ultimate outcome would be. Seeing Musa struggle to hold on to life was a lesson we would never forget. All those who had left us in our short lives were taken suddenly. Watching as a full grown pack member fought for life was something we had not yet experienced.

It took Musa three days to succumb to his injuries. The pack continued to hunt and bring food to those who were injured. The other two dogs healed quickly but Musa became weaker as the days progressed. By the third day, he was too weak to eat. Father fussed over Musa more than I had ever seen him do before. Watching him, it dawned on me that the incapacitated Musa and the other males who had returned were our brothers. Father already grieved over Musa. Seeing him so vulnerable broke my heart.

I made my way over to them and sat next to Father. A small whimper from me drew his attention. He licked my nose and laid next to Musa, making room for me to lay next him. Musa worked up enough energy to lick me as well, I think as a way of reassuring me that everything would be alright. We laid next to him the rest of that night.

Some time during the night, I startled awake, whatever nightmare I'd been having fading quickly from my mind. The pack lay sleeping, oblivious to the night sounds that echoed across the valley. I turned to see Father looking at me. He had been keeping watch as the rest of the pack slept. His eyes showed his mourning and I turned to Musa, who lay unnaturally still. A soft whimper left me as I looked back to Father.

"Yes, little one," Father whispered. "Musa has gone with the others who have left us. He will no longer feel any pain."

I laid my head down and thought of all those who had left us since my birth. So much loss! My heart ached not only for those who had left, but for those who remained behind.

"Mother says that I will leave the pack someday," I said, looking off into the distance. "It is already hard with a pack as big as ours. I can't imagine trying to survive out there on my own."

"Your mother is very wise, M'vita. It is the way of our kind for the females of the pack to leave and find territories and packs of their own. But worry not. They do not do it alone. The sisters band together with the strongest one becoming alpha. The same is true for males who wish to leave the pack. Look at Musa and his brothers. They left home around the time you and your siblings were born. In the end, they came home but there are many times when males will pair up with rogue packs of sisters instead, making their own packs away from home."

I thought about what he had said. It did make sense the way he explained it. It would be quite difficult for a wild dog to survive on their own. When the time came, would Marika, Suri, Zephyr, and I form our own pack? Another thought came to my mind as I considered leaving Sasha, Kanji, and Horu behind.

"Father," I asked, quietly. "Do you think my brothers could leave with us, instead of making two different packs? We are stronger together."

"No, little one. That is not the way. Let's say you are the strongest of your sisters. You become the alpha of your pack. Who would be your mate? Would you chose Sasha, your adventurous brother,

Kanji, the brave one, or Horu, the quiet one who often submits to the rest of you?"

"I would have to chose one of my brothers?"

"If not your brothers, who would your chose? I do not think that they would allow another male to come into your pack and pick up the mantle of leadership, especially Sasha or Kanji."

"I guess you're right. Sasha already tries to bully me. I can't imagine what he would do to someone unrelated."

"Think of it in another way," he continued. "If you were to leave and join Sasha's pack, how would you feel if a female from another pack came in to take up leadership, especially if she were weaker than you?"

"I guess you're right. I never thought about it that way. I just can't imagine leaving everyone behind, particularly my siblings. We have been through so much."

Father chuckled and bumped his nose against my cheek. "Worry not, little M'vita. When the time comes, you will be more than happy to leave.

Sooner or later, Sasha's antics will become too much for you. And who knows, he may even leave before you, taking the decision out of your hands."

"You know, Father. You are wise, too." I smiled up at him and some of his sadness faded. "I'm glad you are my father."

"And I am glad you are my daughter. Some day, you will be a great leader, just like your mother."

I scooted closer to him and he wrapped his long, limber form around me. I slept soundly the rest of the night.

With Musa gone, and the other injured pack members healing, the pack moved on. I was grateful. Being that close to Musa was unsettling for the pack. I often wondered what ever became of the rival pack. Did they perish as well? Fortunately, keeping up with the pack kept my mind busy most of the time and after a while, the fight for survival was enough to keep me focused on what lie ahead instead of what had already passed.

As the dry season reached its peak, even we experienced hard times. Many of the herds migrated across pack lines in search of the last major sources of water. We could not follow and resorted to small prey, such as birds and reptiles. A few times a week we still managed to bring down something larger, usually an old or injured grazer that had been unable to keep up with the rest of its herd.

Just before the rains returned, we had taken down one such grazer. It was a wildebeest. The old male would not have lasted the rest of the season, even if we hadn't brought him down.

We had chased him to the edge of a watering hole that was more mud than water. In fact, I didn't even realize it was a watering hole at first. The wildebeest fought valiantly against us, despite the overwhelming odds. But, he was no match for us. We took him down quickly and began feeding. However, the disturbance did not go unnoticed. Just after felling the beast, as we were focused on feeding, a large crocodile burst from the watering hole.

As I said, I didn't even know it was there. The giant reptile charged us and our kill. A few of the pack members stood their ground, including Sasha and I. Our bellies grumbled from hunger and we did not know when we would eat a hearty meal again. Giving the prey up to the crocodile seemed like such a waste.

Unfortunately, the beast would not relent and gnashed his huge jaws together. The sound echoed through the air and chills ran up my spine. I knew I should back away but my legs were frozen, either from stubbornness or fear. I could not tell which. The rest of the pack barked from a safe distance away, trying to get those of us who had stayed behind to give ground.

The irritable crocodile pushed up onto his legs and charged us. For a split second, all those pack members who had died flashed in my mind. If I didn't move, I could be next. I turned, grabbed Sasha by his scruff, and pulled him away to safety. The others who had stayed behind followed suit. I realized they had only stayed to protect me and my brother. The crocodile grabbed his prize and dragged it into the water. A battle ensued over the carcass and I realized the watering hole was full of crocodiles.

Mother and the rest of the pack ran up to us, whimpering and licking our faces. Mother seemed especially distraught.

"I should have known better," she said, over and over.

"It's alright, Mother," I reassured her. "No one got hurt."

"No, but somebody could have. The rains cannot come soon enough."

As if on cue, just after the sun set, we heard the first rumblings of thunder. My siblings and I had been born after the rains so we had never experienced the brilliance of nature in action. Although the sun had set, the sky lit up with flashes of energy as it raced through thick, black clouds. The energy was so intense, I could feel it seep through me.

Forks of lightning shot from the clouds and headed toward the earth. Before it reached the ground, the earth threw up its own arc of energy and the two met somewhere in the middle. The whole thing happened in a millisecond and I would have missed it had I not been so enraptured by the process. As the storm came closer, the thunder became louder until it accompanied the crashes of lightening. It was both frightening and invigorating. I was introduced to a new kind of energy, born of the earth and sky themselves.

Following close behind the thunder and lightning was the rain. It came down in sheets so thick we could not see a foot in front of us. It also chilled us to the bone. The pack huddled close to each other for warmth and security. The rain was also loud, so loud in fact, we could not hear anything else around us. My greatest hope was that any predators out there were doing as we were, huddled together until the worst of it passed.

Chapter Seven: Renewal

The rains lasted for two months. At first, they fell non-stop for several days. We did not see the sun even once in that time. Neither could we hunt. Not only was the ground too slick to find purchase, the heavy sheets of rain were impossible to see through. The thirsty ground soaked up the water the best it could but as the once dry riverbeds filled to capacity and spilled their banks, the land flooded, sending predators and prey fleeing for higher ground.

We were no exception. Mother found an outcropping high above the flood waters where the pack could rest until the heaviest of the rains subsided. When they finally did, we witnessed a world transformed from a vantage point that allowed us to see far into the distance. I remember the morning like it was yesterday, much like my first sunrise with the pack.

The rains had abated during the night, taking the thunder and lightning with it. The sudden silence woke me from my troubled sleep and I sighed with relief before drifting off once again. The sun woke us the next morning. The wet earth glistened like tiny diamonds for as far as the eye could see. Great bodies of water sat like islands between a drenched world. The land winded around these lakes and rivers, creating passageways for land animals to navigate.

Herds of grazers waded in the water and meandered along the land patches which were already starting to turn green. Zebra, wildebeest, and gazelle frolicked in the early morning and I couldn't help the smile that stretched across my face.

The sky still held heavy grey clouds that threatening rain at any moment but I focused more on the new world around me. Mother watched me and smiled as well. While she had experienced this renewal many times in her life, she knew it was something that would stay with me for the rest of mine.

My stomach grumbled as the rest of the pack woke and stretched out the stiffness in their joints. The small window of opportunity would not last long. If we were going to hunt, we needed to do it soon. We spent a few moments in play, not only to excite our muscles but to warm our bodies in the chilly air. A few moments later, the pack traveled down the outcropping and toward a herd of gazelle.

Navigating around rivers and streams makes hunting difficult. Our prey have long legs so escaping into the water was something they did often. Unfortunately for them, with the sun hidden behind the clouds, the water was cold and only worked to exhaust them more. All we had to do was wait for them to tire enough to retrieve them without risk of injury.

That is how we found a meal on this day. Even the dry ground was saturated. Mud seeped halfway up our legs as we made our way to the herd. My toes tingled from the cold and I wanted nothing more than to find a dry place to rest. But my empty stomach pushed me on.

The herd lifted their heads all together long before we reached them. I think the sound of our feet squelching in the mud gave us away. They took off into the nearest body of water and waded stomach-deep, too deep for us to reach them. The herd was small, only eight individuals and they all watched us with wary eyes and flicking ears. We could have left them and sought out prey elsewhere but Mother knew we would have the same problem. So, she decided to wait them out.

Many minutes passed with the pack surrounding the herd. The agitated gazelle stamped their feet, shooting water high into the air. I could tell they were anxious to leave the cold water. The pack raced back and forth along the bank, agitating the herd further. Father shot out into the water sending the gazelle fleeing for the far side where half the pack waited. The herd split to avoid being caught but one of the smaller gazelles tripped over something under the water. It was all the opening Father needed.

With the gazelle trapped, the pack plunged into the water to drag it to dry land. We did not waste time filling our bellies. Our hunt did not go unnoticed. As I stepped away from the carcass, I could see several sloped bodies heading our way. The rest of the pack filled their bellies and we left the carcass to the scavengers.

"Head back to the outcropping," Mother said. "It is the best place to rest for now."

We did not argue. Already the clouds were building again. I did not want to be on low ground when the rains fell.

By the time the rains ended, the whole of my world had been transformed. We wandered along Mother's territorial lines, keeping to the driest areas as best we could. The land which had once been brown and brittle began to flourish. Green sprouts shot through the baked earth and raced to reach maturity before they could be eaten or trampled. The herd animals gorged themselves on this bounty. The plentiful food meant that our prey was stronger and harder to bring down. But this would soon be overshadowed by an even greater urge, the urge to procreate.

I watched, fascinated, as the huge herd animals fought over territory and females. It seemed so senseless to me, especially considering the females barely seemed to take notice. Zebra bickered and snapped at each other, their calls stretching across the plains and over new-formed lakes. Gazelle slammed their horned heads together. I wondered how they did so without impaling each other.

The buffalo did this as well but the sound of horn smashing against horn reverberated through me, sending chills up my spine. Even the hippos, which dominated the landscape now, fought over mating rites. Their battle was so intense, I couldn't watch it for long.

Probably what was most fascinating and terrifying were the crocodiles. Their mating calls were low and deep and echoed across the water. They would lift up their heads and open their jaws wide. Then they would snap their jaws shut and sink into the water. Little bubbles would rise across their back making a tinkling sound. Then, they would do it all again.

I watched all this while resting between meals. Mother and Father would disappear often during this time so my mind found other things to occupy itself.

Sasha and Kanji seemed equally transfixed and would often sit with me while I watched.

"Herd animals can be so careless," Sasha said one day. "Don't they know they're vulnerable?"

"It's not like they have a choice, Sasha," Kanji answered, rolling his eyes. "If they didn't mate, we would have nothing to eat." Ah, Kanji, always the smart one!

"But look at them! Anything can just come up and grab them while they aren't paying attention."

I sighed and turned to my oldest brother. "They aren't the only ones down there. I can assure you the females are keeping a watchful eye. Even if the males are too preoccupied, the females will protect the herd…like always."

I just had to throw in that last barb. After all, wild dog societies are ruled by females. Both Sasha and Kanji turned to me and I couldn't hide the smirk that stretched across my face.

"You're so full of it!" Sasha yelled and he and Kanji pounced on me.

We rolled around like pups half our age, laughing and enjoying the cool mid-day air. The other dogs in the pack looked on and laughed at our antics. Before long, Zephyr, Suri, and even Horu joined in. Marika chose to sit out. I think she thought herself too mature to indulge in childish games.

A sharp bark from the edge of the clearing had every head turned in that direction. Mother stood looking at us. While she tried to show a stern face, I could see the corners of her lips fighting a smile.

"That is enough play," she reprimanded. "We must all rest before this evening's hunt."

"Yes, Mother," we said in unison. I noticed Marika's smug smirk and stuck my tongue out at her.

Me, Kanji, and Sasha cuddled up together. With the rain clouds gone, the sun beat down relentlessly. Luckily, it was still cool enough not to be a problem, as long as we could find shade. Sasha laid on his belly with his chin on his front legs, once again looking out at the herds.

"Seriously, though, why do you think they invest so much time and energy into it?" he asked. "Why can't they just do it and be done with it?"

"I don't know, brother," I answered. "Maybe one day we will understand. When we are older."

The discussion brought to mind the ones I'd had with Mother and Father. The ones where we were destined to leave the pack.

"You know, there will come a day when we leave this pack," I started. "Then we will be the ones preoccupied with all of that."

"What?" Kanji and Sasha said at once.

"Shhhh!" I whispered, turning quickly to Mother who seemed to be in a conversation with Father. "It's true. Look at the pack. Do we have any older sisters?"

They thought for a moment, looking at each pack member individually. Most of the pack was made up of males of all ages.

"No, I guess not," Kanji answered. "But we have older brothers. And aunts."

"True, but do you remember when Musa and his brothers came back? They had been gone for a long time."

"Yeah, so what," Sasha chimed in. I could already see the dandelions spinning in his head.

"So they left to find their own pack. When they couldn't, they came back."

"So, what you're saying is that we will all leave?" Kanji seemed both frightened and excited.

"Maybe. For sure, me, Marika, Zephyr, and Suri will leave. I think you two will as well. Horu might stay. I can't imagine him being brave enough to leave. But you two are."

"Okay, so when the time comes, we all leave together." Sasha lifted his head and nodded as though he had come up with a brilliant plan.

I shook my head but he didn't seem to notice. Kanji did.

"What is it, M'vita?" he asked, once again getting Sasha's attention.

"We will not leave together. You two will go off to find a wandering pack of females and the rest of us will go off to find a wandering pack of males."

"But...that doesn't make any sense," Sasha argued. "We are stronger together. Why can't we all stay together?"

"I will try to explain it the way Father explained it to me. One of you will be alpha. And one of us girls will be alpha. We cannot both be alphas of the same pack."

"Wait, did you say Father?" Kanji asked.

I chuckled, feeling a little smug that I had uncovered the mystery first. "Yes, Kion is our father and Mother's mate."

We turned to see Mother cuddled with Kion across the clearing. Her head was bowed and I could see a glow reflecting off her form. Whatever he said had her giggling like a she-pup.

"Well, that makes sense," Kanji said.

"I don't want to leave my family," Sasha cried, laying his chin back down.

"Father said when the time comes, you will be ready. For now, just enjoy life and stop asking so many hard questions."

He cut his eye at me and fought to hide his smile. Kanji chuckled and laid his head across my back. Content, I rested my head on my paws and closed my eyes.

Chapter Eight: New Life

With spring came new beginnings. Overall, our first year had been a good one. We fed well and grew quickly. And, after Musa's death, we did not lose anyone else from the pack. The world around us had transformed into a paradise with vibrant green grasses and clear waters. Spring flowers dotted the landscape like the stars did the night sky.

With these new beginnings, came new life. Predators and grazers alike were welcoming a new generation into the world. Watching the grazers give birth was a new experience for me and one that I would never forget. Unlike predators, who usually found a quiet, hidden place to give birth, grazers did so in the open, surrounded by the rest of the herd.

The newborns would find their feet within several minutes and join the rest of the herd. The few memories I had of my earliest days were filled with darkness from eyes that had yet to open. Even when they did open, my siblings and I stumbled along on our bellies or feet that were too weak to hold us up. But the grazers! They were running with the herds within their first day. I know this was because grazers needed to keep moving. A stationary herd was easy prey for predators.

Once the first grazer gave birth, the others followed in quick succession. By the end of the first week, the land was teeming with new life. The newborns frolicked and played amongst the herds, throwing their heads around in the excitement. Even when the pack needed to hunt, the newborns soon returned to their playful nature. I often wondered how the mothers discussed the dangers with their offspring. Many newborns were lost to predators. And yet, they still had such boundless energy.

Not long after the herds began to give birth, Mother would slip away for hours on end. We also traveled more than usual. After a few weeks, We realized what she was doing. The grazers were not the only ones bringing in new life. Mother had been digging dens across her territory for own upcoming arrivals.

One evening, Mother disappeared into one of these burrows. Father paced back and forth in front of the entrance, seemingly lost in his own world. When Mother started to whimper, I jumped to my feet and approached him. He stood tall in front of me and would not allow me passage.

"Mother is hurt!" I cried. "We need to do something."

"There is nothing we can do, youngling," Father said with sad eyes. "This is something only your mother can do."

"I don't understand. We have helped others who have been injured. How can we not help our alpha in her time of need?"

I turned to the rest of the pack. My siblings had gotten to their feet in support of me but the rest had turned from me. I couldn't understand how they could turn on Mother after all she had done for them. More whimpering had me stepping closer to Father. Sasha and Kanji moved to flank me.

"Your mother is giving birth, M'vita, and cannot be disturbed. There is nothing we can do to help her."

My cheeks flamed from embarrassment, as did those of Sasha and Kanji. We backed down and settled next to our other siblings. Mother struggled the rest of the night and well into the next day. The first cry from a newborn pup came with the rising of the sun. I thought that was a good omen.

Mother had given birth to seven pups, four brothers and three sisters. The litter was the smallest she had ever had and there were whispers that her advancing age was the cause. Still, all the pups were healthy and Mother took a well-deserved rest. With the birthing and the danger of her being discovered out of the way, the pack left to hunt, leaving two older males behind to keep an eye out for danger.

After eating our fill, we returned to feed the others. Father barked softly at the den entrance to call for Mother. She crawled out of the small opening and fell on him, her hunger ravenous. Once she was finished, she spent a few minutes in quiet conversation with him before disappearing back into the den.

Mother, being the only one who could nurse the new pups, stayed behind for the next few weeks while the pack hunted. I began to feel the pull that both Mother and Father and told me about. I'm not sure if it was the birth of the new litter or something else but I watched the world with different eyes. I noticed the same thing in my siblings eyes. We were nearly ready to journey out on our own.

Part of me wanted to wait until the younglings emerged from the den. I wanted to say hello to them before never seeing them again. But, I knew it would be weeks before they were able to explore their new world. Already, Sasha, Kanji, and Horu were talking about exploring the far reaches of Mother's territory. I think being cooped up at the den site for so long had began to chafe at their new-found freedom.

One evening, after everyone had gone to sleep, I heard Sasha and Kanji whispering. I knew what they were discussing. Was I ready to lose them, yet? I quietly got to my feet and approached them. As though sensing I was coming, they made room for me. I sat next to them and just looked them in the eyes for a moment.

"You're leaving tomorrow, aren't you?" I asked, moisture filling my eyes.

Kanji nodded. "It's time, sister. With the new pups, the pack has too many mouths to feed. And besides, don't you feel it?"

"But…I'm not ready," I cried, tilting my head to the side. "I'm not ready to never see you again. Take me with you."

"Even you said we couldn't do that," Sasha said softly.

"Not forever," I continued. "Just for a little while. Until we find signs of other packs. Then we can go our separate ways. One year isn't enough, Sasha. You two aren't just my brothers. You're my best friends. I can't do this without you."

Kanji butted his head against mine and licked my nose. My chest shuddered from suppressed sobs and he ran his cheek along mine for comfort, probably both his and mine.

"Come, let's rest," he said. "Tomorrow we will tell the others. It might go against tradition, but I don't see a problem with us sticking together for a little longer. After all, me made our first journey together. It seems fitting that we share our last one together."

Sasha nodded his agreement and we curled around each other. I laid my head against Kanji's chest. His strong, steadfast heartbeat soon lulled me to sleep.

The following morning dawned bright. A rainbow of colors graced a sky littered with puffy clouds. The heat would soon burn them away leaving a gloriously sunny day to begin our journey. We spent one last dawn with the pack. Mother slept within the den nursing the pups. I didn't want to bother her but I also didn't want to leave without saying goodbye. Luckily, we had a little bit of time.

After the morning hunt, Sasha called all of our siblings together. We lagged behind the rest of the pack so we could talk without being heard. Sasha told them of the plan. After returning to the den site, we would let the rest of the pack know we were leaving. They would be losing seven hunters but without the need to feed us, they should do just find. And hunting had been plentiful since the beginning of spring.

"Is there anyone who does not wish to come with us?" Sasha asked. "Horu, I know you can stay if you want. The pack will allow it. But the rest of us need to leave. Be it now or later."

I noticed Marika flinch. I guessed she would be the hardest to convince. She loved the pack and her place in it. I doubt she would ever understand the need for her to leave it. Surprisingly, Horu spoke up first.

"I want to come with you," he said. "I know I will never be an alpha but you have all accepted me for who I am. I would rather stay with you than to try and find a new place within the pack."

Sasha nodded his head and looked around at each of us. Suri and Zephyr nodded in return. Me and Kanji nodded and finally we all turned to Marika. Her legs shook slightly and her ears flicked back and forth.

"Do we have to leave now?" she whimpered.

"It is time," I answered, moving closer to her. "Hunting is good. Mother is preoccupied with the new litter. Soon, they will be wandering around outside the burrow and it will be even harder to leave. Do not worry, sister. We will all be together. At least for a little while."

"Okay." She lowered her head in agreement. "But we have to tell everyone goodbye first, including Mother."

"We will," Kanji answered. "Now let's catch up to the rest of the pack. If we hurry, we can see Mother before she goes back in the den."

We turned for home one last time and stretched our legs out to catch up with the rest of the pack. Once we reached the den, I think the others knew what was coming. Having already fed those left behind, they all stood looking at us. Even Mother had waited to retreat into the den. Sasha, Kanji, and I were in the front of our own little pack. Both Mother and Father approached us, rubbing their faces along ours and licking our noses.

"So, the time has come?" Mother asked. Her face beamed with radiance and pride. "Have you all decided to leave together? Even after our talk?"

"Yes, Mother," I answered, standing tall in front of her. "It is only temporary but we agreed we'd have a better chance if we all stick together. At least for now."

"I am so very proud of you all. You are great hunters and one day, I hope to hear your calls across the grasslands. Be strong. The journey ahead will not be easy. Look out for each other and when the time comes to go your separate ways, make sure that you are ready."

"Yes, Mother!" we all answered in unison.

With her final words, she kissed each of us goodbye, followed by Father. Then, the pack descended on us, each with their own form of farewell. I soaked in the energy from each one, knowing that I would never feel it again. I would miss that most, each dog's individual energy. When the goodbyes were finished, we had worked ourselves up into a frenzy. With one last look at my childhood pack, we turned and sprinted off into the grass.

Chapter Nine: A New Adventure

Our journey took us to the far reaches of Mother's territory. We avoided the border with Shion, not just because of the threat of running into them but also what he had said about the two-legs. The last thing we needed was a run in with them! Instead, we went north. Several days of travel led us to Mother's northern border. The journey filled us with wonder as we watched the brilliance of spring pass us by.

During the day, we only stopped long enough to hunt. I will admit that hunting was a little harder without the full pack behind us but we were all good hunters. We set out early in the morning, just after the sun rose, traveled until dusk, and then sought out our prey. For the most part, we focused on the young grazers, the younglings that had been born just that year. It wasn't as big a meal as we were used to but it was enough for the seven of us.

After eating our fill, we would find a sheltered place to sleep. It was then that we would cuddle and talk about the excitement of the day. For each of us the excitement would be different. Sasha marveled at the vastness of the world. He wanted to conquer it all and rule it as supreme alpha. We chuckled at his pride. Suri said he acted more like a lion lording over his world.

Kanji gushed over the beauty and peacefulness. He expressed his delight at not having come across any other predators on our journey. I knew he wasn't scared. Kanji stood as one of the bravest dogs I'd ever known. But, having to journey around lions and hyenas would slow us down and it would distract us from hunting.

Horu had wide eyes and took in everything as though for the first time. I believed he would eventually break out of his shell and become more confident and strong, especially if he was stuck with Kanji and Sasha.

Suri was as rambunctious as ever. Much like Horu, she looked at the world wide-eyed. However, her look was calculating. She watched the herds move over the grasslands, taking note of their movement patterns. In truth, if not for her observant nature, we most likely would have missed a few meals. Since she kept a close eye on them, we almost always knew where they would be.

Zephyr moved with her head close to the ground. Her large ears picked up sounds even ours couldn't. By listening to the earth, she could tell what the terrain would be like up ahead. We nearly fell into a ravine that had been hidden by bushes but Zephyr's powerful ears and quick reflexes saved us.

The only one I worried about was Marika. She still acted a bit skittish, jumping at every noise and whimpering in her sleep. She missed the comfort and security our large pack had offered her. Even then, by the time we reached the northern border, she had mostly overcome her fear.

We knew we had reached Mother's northern border as soon as we stepped on the line. Although the scent had faded over time, we could still make out the distinct smells of the pack. They would need to refresh them soon to keep out interlopers. We spent our last night on the border, none of us in a hurry to cross over.

That night, we heard our first hyenas since beginning our journey. They chased some animal to ground in a night hunt. By the time we heard them, they were nearly on top of us. The night was particularly dark and we could not see exactly where they were.

Luckily, Zephyr had found us an outcropping to pass the night which put us above the action on the ground. We stayed completely quiet to avoid detection. Although we could not see the hyena's, we knew it was a big pack and we were no match for them. By morning, all that was left of the animal was a few scattered bones.

We watched the last sunrise on Mother's land. It was a bittersweet moment. On the one paw, we would miss it. It had been all we'd ever known and by now, we knew almost every inch of it. On the other paw, the world past the borders beckoned us with a whole new adventure. Sure, there would be danger, and excitement, and a whole world of possibilities. I closed my eyes and breathed in deep.

"Are we ready?" Sasha asked, his eyes glittering.

We all nodded and jumped from the outcropping. With one last look behind us, we crossed the border into no-man's land, forever saying goodbye to our childhood home.

We stayed together throughout the rest of spring and half-way into summer. Although we had moved well past Mother's territory, we did not encounter the scent of any other wild dog's. I wondered what this meant as we made our way over new terrain. While I was grateful to have more time with my brothers, I worried that we would not be able to find our own packs. Little did I know we had moved too close to the two-legs.

I first smelled it near the beginning of summer, just as the grasses were beginning to dry out and the land soaked in the excess water. The strange smell had Marika stopping in her tracks with her head and ears raised high.

"What is it, sister," Sasha asked. By now, we had learned to trust Marika's instincts.

"Do you smell that?" she asked, lifting her nose to take a deeper whiff. "I've never smelled anything like it before."

We followed suit and took a deep breath. I coughed and snorted, trying to remove the burning smell from my nose. The others had similar reactions. Marika lowered her head and followed the scent. After a short walk, we came to a clearing. A strange foreign structure with a peaked roof sat in the middle. It looked almost like a den but was made from leaves and grass.

In front of it was a circle of rocks with something we'd never seen before. It looked a little like the sun except it wouldn't keep its form. It moved and shifted as though it didn't know what shape it was supposed to be. Even as far away as we were, we could feel the heat from it.

Above it sat an animal. At least I think it was an animal. It looked a little like a warthog but it was shriveled and dark. I realized the smell was coming from it. I jumped back.

"We need to leave," I said, my body shaking. "We shouldn't be here. It doesn't feel right."

My siblings had just joined me in the grass when a creature emerged from the den. It was tall, like an ostrich and walked on two-legs. Its furless skin was nearly as dark as the warthog sitting over the shifting sun. Immediately, I realized what it was: a two-legs. We turned and raced away from the clearing. Now we understood why there were no dogs in this land. We would need to keep moving.

That evening, we located the herds. They had been scattered, partly because the water was drying up and partly because the territory we traveled through became more dense with heavy brush and large boulders. I think it was also because of the two-legs which occupied the area.

We surrounded a small, isolated group that had wandered some distance away from the rest of the herd. As one, we charged the group. I had already located a weak female and made my way to her. Despite being weakened, she still managed to outmaneuver me, kicking her back legs out far behind her. The rest of my siblings tried to flank her as I chased her toward a group of boulders.

Somehow, she managed to weave her way through them, causing my siblings and I to get separated. After an exhaustive chase, we finally managed to bring her down. At first, I didn't realize that Marika had yet to catch up. We were nearly finished feeding when I heard a deep bark low to the ground.

I lifted my head and scanned my surroundings but I could not see her. The barking continued and I realized Marika was trying to locate us without catching the attention of any predators that may be nearby.

"Sasha," I called, softly. "Marika is lost. I am going to find her."

"We are done here," he answered. "We will go together."

The others nodded and we turned toward the sound coming from the earth. Every now and then, I would send a call back to her, lowering my nose almost against the ground before sending a bark to her. This was something Mother had taught us as soon as we left the den. She said if we ever got lost or became separated from the pack, it was the safest way to find our way back.

Before long, Marika shot from around a boulder and we fell into a jumble of legs and ears as we welcomed her back. Having missed the meal, we eagerly shared ours with her.

"Let's not do that again!" she said, with a sigh of relief.

"I agree!" we all answered.

While Marika ate, we took a moment to rest. Sasha sat looking out at the land around us. The territory was less than ideal for a wild dog pack to thrive. We all knew this but had no idea of where to go now. I walked up and sat next to him. His ear flicked away a fly and his nose twitched, probably from one of the many strange smells on the wind.

"Do you have any ideas of where we should go from here?" I asked.

"No," he answered. "I just don't have a clue. Everything is so different here. Even the smells are strange."

"What if we followed the sun? If we could find a river, we could follow it until we find less arid land. Something more open where hunting would be easier. And maybe, we can find other dogs."

"Are you so eager to be rid of us?" Sasha cocked his head and grinned at me.

"No," I chuckled, bumping his shoulder.

"For what it's worth, I think you're right. At least near water the herds will be easier to catch. We will rest here for the night and head out tomorrow."

"I will let the others know." I stood up and turned to go but faced him for a moment before stepping away. "And Sasha, I'm in no hurry to tell you goodbye."

He chuckled but didn't turn to me. "Nor I, you, little sister. Nor I."

Chapter Ten: Different Paths

The journey west took us out of the rough terrain and led us to a more open landscape. By the end of the first day, we had located a small river, its banks shriveled to a fraction of its former glory. It trickled along slowly, winding its way through grasses already turning brown. Despite its small size, we decided to follow it, hoping it would lead to a larger body of water.

After two more days of travel, we found what we were looking for. The small river emptied into a large lake surrounded by green grasses and scrub bushes. It was a tiny piece of paradise, an oasis from the heat that offered shelter, food, and water. Animals of all sorts grazed near its banks or hid beneath its waters.

We stopped on a rise just a little ways off and took it all in. A small black-backed jackal skipped along the bank looking for a safe place to drink while a herd of zebra took their fill across from it. From where we were, we could see hippos submerged on one end and the tell-tale signs of crocodiles on the other.

"I think I see a place we can rest," Kanji said, looking off just past the lake. "We may as well stay here for a while until we figure out what we're gonna do."

"That sounds like a good idea," I agreed. "Maybe we can make this our territory for now."

The others nodded and we made our way to a small outcropping of rocks. It provided shelter from the sun and gave us a great viewpoint of the whole floodplain.

That evening we hunted. Although the herds scattered, they did not leave the area. I guessed they valued the source of water too much to try to avoid predators. Once we were fed, we returned to the outcropping.

"This could work," Sasha said once we were all resting. "The rainy season is only a few weeks away and yet, there is still so much water. I don't think this lake disappears like the others. And if there is water, there is food."

"What about other dogs?" Horu asked. Usually he was the quiet one. His question had us all turning our heads to him.

"Well, I didn't sense any during our hunt," Sasha answered. "But, if they make their way here like we did, we may be able to form the packs we need. And if not, we will continue on once the rains return."

That did make the most sense. For the time, we were better off staying where we knew we were safe instead of trekking out into the unknown. With the decision made, we curled up together and fell asleep.

Sometime during the night, we were awakened by the roars of lions. They were far too close for comfort and we realized they had probably come to the oasis for the same reason we did. If not for our shelter, I'm certain they would have found us. We would need to be even more vigilant when we hunted.

The next few weeks passed easier than those that had come before it. Despite the presence of the lions, we lived and hunted in relative peace. We kept our distance from them and when we hunted, we ate quickly. By the time they found our carcass, we were already gone. Near the end of summer, a pack of hyenas joined the lions. The scavengers followed the big cats everywhere they went, which meant they left us alone.

Just before the rains returned, we had our second encounter with the two-legs. Being just the seven of us, we only needed to hunt once a day, which we did in the evenings. The rest of the day we rested. In truth, it was too hot to do much else anyway. At dawn, just before the sun peaked over the horizon, we made our way to the lake to drink.

At this time, most of the other predators slept and would not be a threat to us. Once we satisfied our thirst, we returned to the outcropping to sleep off the heat of the day. On this particular day, I was restless, despite the soaring heat. Kanji, who lay nearest me, also seemed restless. My other siblings lay on their sides, panting to keep cool.

"Do you feel that?" I asked Kanji, keeping my voice soft enough to not bother the others.

He lifted his head and turned to me. "Yes, but I don't know what it is."

I was sitting up on my belly looking off into the distance. The feeling I had wasn't a physical thing. It wasn't like the air or the ground around me. It wasn't even like the energy I felt from my siblings. This feeling came from deeper inside me, as though my body were anticipating something that had yet to happen.

"I wonder what it is?" I said, my ears perked for any sound that might pierce the quiet of the day.

"Are you anxious?" Kanji asked. "When the rains come, we will leave. We may even find other wild dogs."

"Well, I won't lie. I am a little. What we have right now is so comfortable. I can't imagine leaving it all behind. And what happens if we do find other packs and they don't accept us? It has been several months since we left Mother's land and we haven't found any evidence of other packs. What do you think the odds are that we will find lone packs of males or females so late in the season?"

Kanji sat up as well and bumped his nose against my cheek. "If that happens, then we will just have to stick together until the rains pass and new younglings branch out on their own. We will find them eventually. The world is only so big."

"I guess you're right. Sometimes I wonder if we left Mother's pack too soon. Maybe, if we had just stayed a little longer, we would have had a better chance."

"Mother's pack was already too big, even when we were pups. With the new litter, there was no way we could have stayed. Besides, we have done well so far. We haven't lost anybody, and that is saying something, and we are all strong and healthy."

I leaned against Kanji's shoulder and closed my eyes. "You're such a great brother. It's a shame you don't want to be alpha. I think you would make an excellent leader."

"Nah, I'm happy just being an advisor. I don't want all that responsibility."

"Whatever!" I laughed, bumping against him before pulling away. "We'll see what happens."

Suddenly, the ground beneath us rumbled. It was soft at first and barely caught our attention but as it increased, we turned worried eyes to each other.

"Sasha," I yelled, waking my oldest brother. "Horu, Suri, Zephyr, Marika! Wake up!"

My siblings jumped to their feet even before they were fully awake. I looked around the floodplain trying to find the source of the rumbling. Usually, if an especially large herd were spooked, they could cause the ground to rumble when they stampeded. If the herds were stampeding close enough for us to feel it, then we could be in danger.

As I looked around, however, the herds were calm. Despite this, the rumbling only increased. My siblings and I began to panic. If we didn't know where it was coming from, we couldn't run from it. Suddenly, from behind the outcropping, came an animal I'd never seen before. It was large, like a rhino or a hippo and moved in a way that its feet never left the ground. It was also made of sharp edges, like rock. It rumbled over the ground kicking up a dust cloud behind it.

Hoping to avoid detection, we lowered ourselves to the ground. There was no way we could outrun it.

And we didn't even know if it was a predator or not. Usually, things that big were grazers and meant us no harm. Then again, things that big usually traveled in herds.

We lay perfectly still as the animal approached. At first, we thought it was going to simply pass by us. We were not so lucky. It ground to a halt near our hiding spot making a noise that sounded painful to me. Its eyes still faced forward and it did not turn its head so I still held out hope that it hadn't seen us.

Then, it did something I'd only ever seen once before. As a pup, when we still lived in the den, there was a cluster of scrub brush near the edge of the den sight. In the brush lived a spider, or several, actually. One time, while watching the spiders, I noticed babies crawling out of the back of one of them. Mother said it was how the mother spider kept her babies safe. She called them wolf spiders.

Well, the animal in front of us was not a wolf spider and the things that crawled out of it looked nothing like it. But the way they tumbled from it reminded me of the mother spider, nonetheless. In fact, it was almost as if the animal regurgitated them, much like how we regurgitate our food for those unable to hunt.

After the initial shock passed, I realized the things that came from it were two-legs. Unfortunately, I came to this realization too late. I jumped up to run, calling for my siblings as I did. Before I could disappear into the grass, I felt a sting in my thigh. I didn't get far before oblivion found me.

I don't know how much time passed before my groggy brain began to function again. I remember a swaying feeling beneath me, like I was floating on air and a loud rumbling beneath my ear. The more aware I became, the more I noticed the jolting of the ground below me. I opened my eyes and blinked back the blurriness. I was in some type of den except the walls were unnaturally straight. Night had fallen and I could see no light at all. I could not even see an opening for the den.

Immediately, I looked around for my siblings but I was all alone. The ground beneath me was moving and my stomach twisted at the sensation. Lowering my nose to the floor of the den, I called for my siblings. Right away I heard my sisters. They were close.

"Sasha," I called but received no answer. Maybe he was not yet awake. "Kanji! Horu!" Still no answer. Could they all still be sleeping?

"I do not think they are here, M'vita," Zephyr called. "I have been awake for a while and have not heard them even once."

Panic filled me. What had the two-legs done to my brothers? What are they planning to do to us?

"We have to stay calm," I tried to reassure Zephyr, Suri, and Marika, even though my own voice shook. "The first chance we get, we make a run for it and we all stay together."

They mumbled their agreement. The swaying of the den made me ill to my stomach and I lay down on the floor. My mouth felt dry and I desperately wished for some water. With nothing else to do, I closed my eyes and let sleep once again claim me.

We traveled for a couple of days in the moving dens. The morning following our capture, the ground stopped moving for a short time. My stomach welcomed this and I was finally able to stand up without falling over. Something shook the ground for a moment and then all was still.

Without warning, the roof of my den was lifted. At least, I thought it was the roof. Sunlight streamed into the den, blinding me for a moment. When my eyes adjusted, I realized I wasn't in a den. It was more like a thorn bush, only without the thorns. It was covered with some type of skin to keep out the sun. Just past the walls were three two-legs. Two of them were as pale as summer grass. The third was as dark as night.

The first pale one had a mane the color of rich soil that fell past its shoulders and disappeared down its back. Eyes the color of the sky peered in at me. It lifted its lips to show me its teeth. Was it trying to threaten me with such small teeth? I backed up, just in case.

The other pale one had a mane of gold like the sun. The mane was much shorter than the first pale one and I wondered if it were just younger, like that of a lion. However, it was much bigger than the first one, in both height and weight. It, too, had sky-colored eyes but they were much lighter and more brilliant. In fact, it was almost mesmerizing. Neither had fur on their faces.

The dark-skinned two-legs reminded me of the one we had seen on our travels. It was dark from head to toe with black eyes. Its mane was shorter than the pale ones and it wore a strange, colorful decoration upon its head. It smiled as well and its blunted teeth were as white as sun-bleached bones.

The golden-maned two-legs approached the thornless bush while the dark-skinned one poured water into them. I wanted the water so badly but the two-legs were too close.

"It is alright, little one," the golden-haired two-legs said, even though I did not understand his words. "We are taking you to a new home, *un paradis,* where you can find others like yourself and where you will be safe. We have even brought your sisters with you."

The two-legs pointed to the other bushes where Zephyr, Suri, and Marika rested. I understood at least part of his meaning. I barked back, asking him about my brothers.

As if it could understand, it said "Your brothers were taken somewhere else where they, too, could start new. The seven of you were far too close to human lands. It was not safe for you there, *bel enfant.*"

His soothing voice calmed me and even though I didn't understand him, I realized he meant us no harm. When he stepped away, I rushed to the water and filled my parched throat. The two-legs chuckled and replaced the cover over my "den".

I heard my sisters in their own enclosures doing the same. In the back of my mind, warning bells were ringing. All my life I had been told to beware of the two-legs. They were dangerous. But for some reason, I did not fear these ones. At least not as much as I should have. And why did they separate us from our brothers? Would I ever see them again? As I lay back down to endure more of the moving ground, I realized I didn't even get a chance to tell them goodbye.

Chapter Eleven: Oasis

We reached our new home just after dawn on the third day. The two-legs moved our enclosures onto the ground one at a time. They left the covers on them until all four enclosures were next to each other. I could smell the grass and water, even through the cover. When the two-legs pulled them off, I was greeted with a sight I would never forget.

My most memorable sunrise was the one I shared with the whole pack in my childhood because of the energy each dog added to it. This sunrise would be the second most memorable one because of the sheer beauty of it.

We were on a rise, surrounded by rolling hills and tall green grasses that the summer heat had not yet killed off. In the distance was a huge lake that glistened with the brand new sun. At the farthest end of my field of vision was a mountain that stood above everything else around it. Distance alone made it seem tiny in my eyes but I knew if I stood at its base, I would not be able to see its peak. Large swaths of forest bordered the edges of the horizon and the base of the mountain.

As the sun rose, I began to see animals. Large herds of antelope, some of which I'd never seen before, meandered through herds of wildebeest and zebra. Near the water were buffalo and hippo. Everything seemed so unreal and peaceful. A trumpet off to my right had my head turning in that direction. A small herd of elephants were making their way to the lake.

Once the shock wore off, the two-legs lifted the doors of our enclosures. We did not waste any time. Before we could second guess our decision, we shot out of the enclosures and into the grass. I'm almost certain I heard the two-legs laugh as we disappeared.

My sisters and I ran until our breathing became ragged and our legs began to ache. After all, we had been cooped up in a small enclosure for a couple of days. By the time we stopped, we had reached the flood plains near the lake. We stood at the edge and took everything in.

For the most part, this area was open with tall green grasses. Where we had stopped grew trees and scrub brush, enough to allow us protection while we recovered. As we sat to rest, a warm breeze drifted over me, carrying with it a scent I had been longing for.

"Do you smell that?" Suri asked, jumping to her feet.

"I sure do," I answered. "Dogs!"

Somewhere in this vast oasis was a pack of dogs. Whether they accepted us or not was a worry for another day. Together, we set out to find them.

It took us two days to find the pack. During that time, we traversed our new home. It was obvious we were in the pack's territory. Their scent was everywhere. Still, actually finding them proved elusive. We learn why that first night. The roar of a lion echoed through the dark. It was not terribly close but it was inside the pack's territory. Like always, we laid low, hoping the big cat would not find us.

Our second day, we followed a fresh trail straight to where the pack was resting. In fact, we stumbled on them by accident. They had taken refuge under a large tree, seeking shelter from the worst of the summer heat. While following the scent, we had agreed the same tree would be a good place to rest until the sun set.

As we broke through the grass, the pack jumped to their feet, startled by our sudden appearance. There were a few moments of standoff before curiosity got the better of us. As luck would have it, the pack was made up of young males.

"Who are you?" one of them asked.

"M'vita," I answered. "These are my sisters, Suri, Zephyr, and Marika."

"What are you doing here?" asked the same one.

"Well, that's rude," Suri snapped.

"It's alright, Suri," I soothed. "I can handle this. We were brought here by the two legs. Who are you?"

"I'm Kal," he said. "This is Aahi, Soka, and Yuri. And you are in our territory."

"We didn't mean to intrude," I said, taking a step toward Kal. Given his bravado, I assumed he was the leader. "This is where the two-legs left us and we are in search of a pack."

"You have to forgive my brother," Yuri said, stepping forward. "He likes to think he is in charge. You can stay with us, if you'd like."

Yuri reminded me instantly of Kanji and I felt my eyes tearing up. "That would be great."

We spent the rest of the afternoon talking and getting to know each other. Yuri and I hit it off right away. Turned out that *he* was the leader and they had been on their own for two summers, making them a year older than me and my sisters. When I asked why they hadn't formed a full pack yet, he said there weren't any unrelated females anywhere in the oasis and the land was too rich to leave.

That evening, the eight of us left to hunt as a pack. It was the first time I had ever hunted with anyone other than my siblings or extended family. Surprisingly, we worked well together, as if we had always hunted as a pack. After bringing down a large gazelle, we ate quickly and left the rest for the scavengers.

"One thing you have to know about this place is that the lions rule over everything," Yuri said as we made our way to a place to rest for the night. "We have lost many dogs to them and they outnumber us."

"We've lost dogs to lions, too," I said. "We generally give them a wide berth."

"Yeah, well, there are two prides that live in the oasis. The first one, and the largest one, lives near the lake. They follow the herds as they move around the floodplain. The second pride is to the north, closer to the mountain. It has two males and they are more aggressive. The land up there is more arid so near the end of summer, like now, most of the herds move here for water. This puts the two prides in close proximity and sometimes, they fight."

"I heard a lion roaring on our first night here."

"That would be Ibada. He is the leader of the local pride. He was probably reminding the other pride to stay away. The rains are late this year and everyone is on edge. If we stay away from them, they will leave us alone. It is the northern pride that is dangerous."

"I'll have to remember that. Everything is so different here."

Yuri bumped his shoulder against mine and smiled. "You'll get used to it. This place will give you everything you'll every need. Someday, maybe after the rains have come and gone, I'll take you to see Halili. She is the matriarch of the elephants and has been here for six decades. She can tell you all about Paradise."

"Paradise?"

He chuckled. "That is what she calls this land. When I first set out on my own, I would go to see her and listen to her tales for hours. You will love her."

"I can't wait," I sighed and leaned against him. All the excitement had my eyes drifting shut and before I knew it, my head fell across his back.

He chuckled again, the rumble vibrating against my cheek. "Get some sleep, M'vita," he said, licking the top of my head. "Tomorrow, I will show you my world."

True to his word, the next day Yuri and his brothers led us across his territory. The area was huge, even bigger than my mother's territory had been. Most of it was open grassland where the herds grazed. It also included the lake and the area around it. I couldn't understand how a pack of four brothers had been able to hold such a large territory.

"My mother's pack is the only other pack in Paradise and they live on the northernmost border. She never ventures this far south. Actually, we found this place by accident. The northern border is mostly forest with trees so dense you can barely see through them. After leaving my mother's pack, my brothers and I headed south. We knew there was another pack north of Mother's and wanted to avoid them.

"Unfortunately, we ran into two-legs. While running from them, we entered the forest. There are things there I'd never seen before and it was so loud.

We couldn't even figure out where all the sounds were coming from but it sounded like the trees were yelling at us. We just kept running. Eventually, we reached the other side and found this place. We continued south until we reached the lake. We have been here ever since."

"Wow!" I didn't know what else to say.

"Yeah, it's pretty nice. We have plenty of food and water and as long as we stay away from the lions, we are safe."

"My brothers and me and my sisters traveled together for a long time after leaving my mother's pack," I said, suddenly missing Sasha, Kanji, and Horu.

"You left with your brothers?" Yuri seemed shocked by my admission.

"We thought it would be better to stick together for as long as possible. And, I wasn't ready to leave them yet."

"Wow! I've never heard of that before. Mother said that my sisters had to leave on their own. Of course, by the time we left, only two of my sisters were still alive."

"Yeah, my mother was a little shocked when we told her, too. But we traveled throughout most of spring and summer and never found any evidence of other dogs. I wonder if Sasha, Kanji, and Horu returned home?"

"Who knows? But from the way you talk about them, I bet they are still out there, toughing it out. You speak very fondly of them."

"You're probably right. Sasha is too stubborn to go home. Maybe the two legs brought them to a place like this one."

"Maybe. It would make sense. When the rains come, and it starts to cool down, I can take you around the rest of Paradise. It's too hot right now and much of the outlying areas don't have water."

"I would like that." I bumped against him and smiled. "Thanks, for taking us in."

Yuri looked at me curiously and cocked his head. Something was going through his head, something he was thinking really hard about. He turned away for a second and flicked his ear. I sat still, not wanting to interrupt his thoughts but my curiosity had me biting my lip. Finally he turned back to me. He glanced quickly at the others who were deep in their own conversations.

"M'vita..." he started and lowered his eyes. "Would you consider...being alpha with me?" He wouldn't look at me and his ear flicked nervously.

I stood up and approached him, rubbing my body along his. "I would love to, Yuri," I said.

He jumped back and spun in a circle. "Wow! Just...wow!"

I chuckled and settled down to rest. He curled up next to me and rested his chin on my back.

"We're gonna be great together," he said. "Before long, we'll have this whole place filled with new wild dog packs."

"One day at a time, Casanova. And we have plenty days to look forward to."

Chapter Twelve: Halili

A few days later, the rains finally came. Just like the first time, we mostly sat out, waiting for the worst of them to pass before attempting to hunt. Yuri led us to a rise that overlooked most of his territory. There was a cave situated on the very top that allowed us to stay dry.

I watched in amazement as the land flooded, starting with the area around the lake. The rivers that snaked off the lake bulged and spilled their banks, carrying water far past where I could see. The herds moved out as well to avoid the quickly rising water. Watching from our vantage point was a new experience for me.

After a few days, the rains lessened and we were able to hunt and start exploring more of Yuri's territory. He also needed to remark his boundaries. With such a large territory, he needed to remark it often.

He led us north. With the rains, it was safer to travel that way. Not only would the land not be flooded, but many of the herds migrated there to wait out the worst of it. I worried about the lions Yuri kept talking about.

"The lions shouldn't be a problem," he reassured me. "With the herds here, they will be more focused on them than on us. Besides, we will not be here for long. I'm taking you somewhere special."

Intrigued, I followed along with the rest of the pack following behind us.

We traveled for several days, some of it through the rain. Yuri knew the best route to avoid flooding and we zigzagged across his territory. The cooling rains did make the trip a bit easier. After about a week of traveling, we came to the edge of his western border.

Large trees dotted the landscape and became more dense the further west we traveled. In fact, we were quite close to the mountain that I had seen the day we arrived. It was still some distance away but I could sense its massive size even from where we were. I was about to ask Yuri if it was part of his territory when I heard the trumpet of an elephant.

My head whipped around trying to locate it. It wasn't unheard of for a bull elephant to trample a wild dog, especially during mating season.

"Relax, *mpendwa*," Yuri soothed. "This is my surprise."

"You do realize elephants are dangerous?" I chastised.

"Not these ones," he said, smiling. "Come, Halili is probably resting near the watering hole."

I remembered his promise about taking me to see the old matriarch. Having never been that close to an elephant, much less a matriarch, I was both scared and intrigued. But, I trusted Yuri and followed behind him. The rest of the pack stayed back, laying down on the damp grass.

Halili was just where Yuri thought she would be. She was laying down on her stomach next to the watering hole watching a few younglings play and frolic in the water. A handful of adults joined them, either to cool off or just for the sheer joy of it. Yuri barked softly to get her attention.

Her huge ears fanned out as she turned her head around. For a split second, I thought she was going to call out an alarm but she simply flashed him a smile. For an elephant her age, I had never seen such stunted tusks before. I quickly looked at the other elephants and found that all of them had small tusks.

"Well, hello, Yuri," she drawled. Her voice was scratchy with age. "What brings you all the way out here?"

"Hello, Halili!" he answered, moving closer to her. "I wanted you to meet M'vita, my mate. She has been eager to hear your stories."

The old matriarch chuckled. "Well, come closer, child. I don't bite."

"Hello, Halili," I said, moving up closer to Yuri.

Halili reached out with her trunk and ruffled our heads.

"Awe, come on!" Yuri admonished. "I'm not a kid anymore."

"To someone my age, you are." Halili chuckled again. "Come sit next to me, M'vita, and I will tell you all about Paradise, starting with when it was full of every kind of animal. There was once a time that you couldn't move across the plains without bumping into someone and the elephants of old had tusks so long, they would cross over in front of your trunk."

Yuri bumped his head against mine. "I'll be with the rest of the pack. Enjoy your time with Halili."

I nodded and watched as he disappeared through the brush. Turning, I moved closer to Halili and sat just in front of her so that I could watch her as she told her tales.

"It all started three generations ago," she began, her eyes taking on a faraway look. "I was just a babe then. I remember my mother was the matriarch. I had to crane my neck back to see all of her, she was so big. Her tusks could pull whole trees down if she wanted to. But when she ran her trunk over my head, it was feather soft. Our herd was the largest in Paradise and only one of eight. I never even knew how many were in our herd.

"We traveled from one watering hole to another as the land became dry. The plains were full of animals, gazelle of all kinds, buffalo, zebra, wildebeest, giraffe, and the predators like hyenas, lions, cheetahs, leopards, wild dogs. My mother told me it was the most diverse place in all of the world. Of course, I didn't understand what that meant at the time.

"We lived in harmony with the world around us. Sure, the predators took some. But, when the predators died, they became food for others, such as the scavengers and then, they were welcomed back into the earth where they became the food that we ate. It was a great circle and we lived in joy and happiness."

She stopped her story for a moment and looked away.

"What happened?" I asked, already deep into her story.

"The two-legs came," she answered.

I'm sure I saw a spark of anger in her eye but it was gone before I could know for sure.

"At first, we avoided them. At least, as best we could. They weren't even here for us. Unlike most animals, two-legs fight and kill each other seemingly without any reason. Even lions, who occasionally kill

without reason, do not prolong it. But the two-legs…
They were different.

"They came into Paradise carrying sticks that
sounded like thunder and created fire. They would
point them at each other and then they would fall,
never to get up again. The plains were littered with
them so much, that we could not easily navigate
around them.

"We moved further into Paradise but there were
too many of us. After some time, the two-legs began
pointing their thunder sticks at us. We panicked and
tried to leave but there were so many of them and
really, we had nowhere else to go.

"The two-legs stayed in Paradise for many, many
years. By the time they left, the land was but a shell
of what it once was. Almost all of the herd animals
were gone, eaten or killed for sport. The elephants
were targeted for their tusks. Those with the largest
tusks were targeted first. After a generation of this,
there were no elephants left with large tusks.

"With the herd animals mostly gone, the predators began to die off. At least, those not killed by the two-legs. All of the giraffe and zebra were gone, as well as cheetahs, leopards, almost all big cats, in fact. And the wild dogs. Paradise itself was razed, the plains blackened by still smoldering fires.

"It would take another generation for the land to begin to heal. Surprisingly, another kind of two-legs would step in to help. They brought animals that were either gone or in small numbers back to Paradise. I was one of only a handful of elephants who survived. The two-legs brought new elephants to Paradise. The younglings you see now, are the largest number we have had in a season for the last generation.

"Some of the gazelle, buffalo, and hippos were brought from other lands, as well as a new pride of lions and now, even wild dogs. There are still many animals that never returned to Paradise, like most of the big cats and giraffe. And the danger from the two-legs is still here. While we are mostly protected by them, I have seen some move through with their thunder sticks, taking animals however they want. Be very careful, little one. I fear, one day, they will come back and finish what they started."

I looked over at the carefree elephants playing in the water, most of them born after the disaster from a generation ago. Being so long-lived, Halili remembered the devastation as though it happened yesterday and I could tell it still haunted her.

"Despite everything," I said, "Paradise is beautiful. Maybe, it can return to its former splendor. Even though I was not born here, it has become my home. I would never want to leave it."

Halili smiled and I could feel the ground rumbled from her soft laugh. "Aww, to be young again. Perhaps you are right. You and Yuri will usher in a new generation of wild dog. In truth, I have not seen any wild dog pups in more than 20 years. When you have your first litter, and they are old enough to travel, bring them to me. I would love to tell them stories."

"I will!"

"Speaking of stories, visit me again and I will tell you more cheerful stories from before the time of the two-legs. For now, I think your pack is getting restless."

I looked to the sky and realized dusk had fallen without me even realizing it. We needed to take the break from the rains to hunt. I stood up and shook out my fur.

"Thank-you so much, Halili," I said. "It was a great honor to meet you and I hope to see you again soon."

"Me, too, child. It does my heart good to see you and I can tell that Yuri adores you. He is a good dog and a great alpha."

"That he is."

I ran off into the brush and found the pack pacing on the other side. When they saw me, they gathered around, covering me in licks and wagging tails. I shared their enthusiasm as we built up the energy needed for a successful hunt. Once we were fully energized, we took off to find dinner.

Chapter Thirteen: A New Generation

The rains came and went, ushering in a new time of renewal. The eight of us formed a tight-nit pack that hunted and moved as one unit. With the cooler air, we traversed Yuri's territory with ease and comfort, remarking territorial boundaries. Yuri said he had never had a problem with other dogs but he felt the need to reestablish his lines anyway.

Like my childhood home, the rains transformed Paradise. I didn't think it could get more beautiful than it already was. I was wrong. The land turned a vibrant green for as far as the eye could see and my nose filled with the smell of fresh grass. It was also a time of rebirth. New life came to Paradise, the same as it had when I was younger.

Yuri and I often slipped away from the rest of the pack for a few moments alone. He loved showing affection and handled me with the greatest of care. It was during this time that I formed a bond with him unlike any I had ever experienced before. He became my whole world, and I became his.

I never understood what Mother meant when she referred to a mate as a life partner. She said it would be a dog that would complete me, that would fill a piece of me I never knew was missing. This type of partner only came once in a dog's life and even then, most dog's never experience it. After the rains abated and I grew closer to Yuri, I finally understood what she meant.

A few weeks after the first of the grazers gave birth, I realized I would soon be bringing my own pups into the world. An overwhelming survival instinct took over and I began to dig frantically. Thinking back to my mother, I knew I was going to need several dens, in case I ever had to relocate the pups.

The rest of the pack indulged me, even if they didn't fully understand my need to stop for several hours just to dig a den. I think Yuri may have told them what was going on. Either way, after a couple weeks, I had enough dens scattered throughout the territory that I finally felt I could take a moment to rest.

One evening, shortly after finishing the last den, we all lounged on a rise overlooking the lake. I think it may have been one of the first places my sisters and I had stood when first coming to Paradise. The pack sat, content with full bellies, as the sun finished its descent. They spoke softly among each other, occasionally laughing at a joke Soka made. Sadly, we didn't laugh because they were funny so much as they were ridiculous.

Yuri and I sat just a little off to the side watching everyone else. My stomach bulged both from dinner and from the upcoming arrivals. Already, I could feel them moving around. Yuri nuzzled me every now and then, causing me to chuckle.

"Wait…okay, what about this one," Soka said after an exasperated sigh from Zephyr. "What is something everyone has, but no one can lose?"

"Soka, I'm no good at riddles," she cried. "Especially when they don't make any sense."

"It's a shadow," answered Aahi.

"Hey, Aahi!" Soka snapped. "That's not fair. You've already heard that one before."

"Soka, I've heard all your riddles before."

"Of course you have. I wasn't wanting *you* to answer."

Marika and Suri looked at each other and started laughing. "Sasha!" they cried in unison.

"Alright, I have one more that I bet none of y'all know," Soka huffed, his chest pushed out. "Past mountain, meadow, field, and hill I follow the river while standing still."

I watched as everyone stopped to consider the answer. Well, everyone except Kal. I knew what was about to happen and braced myself for the backlash.

"A bank," he said and smirked at an indignant Soka.

"How did you…?" Soka began.

"Because I was the one that first told it to you."

Kal laughed as Soka lunged for him. A smile stretched across my face as I watched them. Kal tended to be the most serious of everyone and it was rare to see him just relax and have fun. Listening to his laughter now brought a warmth to my heart.

"Thank-you," Yuri whispered in my ear.

"For what?" I chuckled and turned to him.

"This. All of it. Ever since we left our home, we have been lost and floundering. When you and your sisters came, you brought with you joy and happiness. You filled our lives with purpose, meaning. Kal, especially, has been overburdened with caution and responsibility, even though I'm the alpha. It's good to see him laugh again."

I leaned into him and closed my eyes. "You're welcome. I'm glad we found you."

The others began to calm down for the night and snuggled close together. The night was a little chilly and the added warmth of bundled dogs kept everyone from getting chilled. Apparently, all was forgiven.

The following week, the puppies came. The pack jostled around, preparing for the day's hunt when I felt pain race across my back. It disappeared as quickly as it came so I pushed it off as though nothing had happened. We went on our hunt as usually, the pain forgotten. Just after bringing down a young gazelle, the pain returned with a vengeance. I didn't even have the strength to eat.

Yuri noticed something was wrong as everyone else ate their fill.

"M'vita, are you all right?" he asked, concern etched across his face.

"I need to get back to the den," I answered, my breath coming in short puffs.

"Kal!" Yuri called for his brother. "Get the pack together as soon as they're finished and meet us at the den."

Kal nodded and turned to deliver the message. I briefly noticed Suri lift her head in concern before Yuri ushered me away.

The next several hours were a blur. I know the pack returned at some point only by the shuffling of their feet outside the den. Yuri never left the entrance. I know he wanted to be next to me. Every whimper had him poking his nose through the entrance asking if I was okay. By daybreak the following morning, it was all over. We had six brand new pups in our pack.

I stayed with them for the first couple weeks, only leaving the den to eat and get water. Yuri beamed every time he heard them or whenever I would leave the den. I knew he waited anxiously for them to be able to leave the den so that they could meet the rest of the pack. Actually, everyone eagerly waited for that moment.

Three weeks after their arrival, the time finally came. Truth be told, we could not have kept them in the den even if we had wanted to. I was out with the rest of the pack when they first emerged. Marika had chosen to stay behind to keep an eye out while the rest of us left. I heard her barks even before we reached the den.

"You little monsters better get back in there and stay there!" she chided. "You're mother will have my head if she comes back and sees you all out of the den."

"But, aunt Marika, we're bored."

Although I could barely hear the tiny voice, I knew it was Toko. He was my "Sasha" and the very image of my older brother, both in appearance and personality. I signaled for the rest of the pack to hang back while I tiptoed up behind the pups. Marika noticed me and just smirked at Toko.

The little pup was the oldest of the litter and had an adventurous heart but he knew that look meant trouble. He slowly turned his head around to see me staring down at him. He yelped and made to run for the den but I blocked it. He and his siblings stood paralyzed.

"So," I said, casually. "I guess this means you're all ready to meet the rest of the pack?"

Their ears perked up and their tails wagged so hard their bodies shook. "Yes, Mother!" they cried all together.

I called out to the others who had held back and they came running from the grass. It was a glorious moment and reminded me of when I had been introduced to the rest of my pack. I sat back and watched the play between the older dogs and the pups, contentment filling my heart.

"Little monsters," Marika joked, laughter bubbling from her belly.

"Weren't we all?" I said.

The next several weeks were mostly uneventful. Paradise flourished, giving us plenty to eat and security. Nothing bothered us and we never had to move den sites, even though I had made plenty. Deep down, the scars from my childhood haunted me. I feared having to move den sites with the pups being so young. Luckily, the lack of predators kept us from having to do so.

Every day, a different dog would stay behind to guard the pups. Most of the time, everything went fine. The pack tolerated the pups and their antics, or more accurately, Toko's antics. But one dog had an especially hard time.

On this day, the rotation fell on Kal. Every dog has a choice on whether or not to stay behind so I was somewhat surprised when Kal said he would do his duty and babysit. The hunt went faster than usual and we returned to the den site ahead of schedule. As we approached, a deep yelp pierced the air followed by growling and laughing. I turned worried eyes to Yuri.

"Uh-oh," I said, and sprinted for the clearing.

Kal lay on his back buried in puppies. They nipped at his ears, tail, and feet while he wiggled and squirmed beneath them.

"Would you stop that!" he cried. "I told you I surrender! Yes, you are good hunters. Now, get off!"

I couldn't help it. I burst out laughing. The sound caught the pups attention and they ran for me. Kal rolled over onto his belly and gave me a sly smile. Of course, he let them win.

My favorite memory of that time, however, had to be about the time I was weaning the pups. They were just over five weeks old and I had been spending less time with them, delegating other pack members to watch over them instead. The separation left the pups feeling upset and abandoned. Yuri took them under his paw, ensuring them that my behavior was necessary for them to grow big and strong.

I lay on the outer fringes of the clearing listening to him as he gathered them all together. By now, they knew he was their father. Unlike my mother, I told them who their father was, especially considering at one point, they thought it was Kal. I laughed so hard when they asked me if it was Yuri's sour brother.

"What if I tell you a bedtime story," Yuri said to the pups. "Would that make you feel better?"

All six heads bobbed in agreement.

"Okay," Yuri began. I listened closely. Yuri's stories fascinated me as much as I knew they would the pups. "A long time ago, when the land was still vibrant and plentiful, wild dogs roamed far and wide. You could hear different packs barking from one end of the world to the other.

"One pack called themselves the Maisha pack. It was during this time that the land began to change. A new creature had come to the land. The dogs, and all the other animals, did not know if they were predators or prey. They didn't possess the tools of a hunter, such as claws and sharp teeth. Nor did they have the size or speed of prey. To many, it seemed like this new creature would fail to adapt to our world and would either leave on their own or simply die off as many weak species do.

"However, this new species did neither. They began to hunt as predators without the natural weapons of other species. So adept were they, that they were even able to hunt other predators. And they did, in great numbers. The Maisha pack believed that they could reason with this new species. After all, the creatures were upsetting the balance, decimating whole packs of dogs and other predators, as well as prey. Perhaps they did not understand the impact they were having on the land.

"The Maisha pack decided to approach these hunters to try to reason with them. The other wild dogs hid in their dens or scattered to the four winds. But the brave dogs of the Maisha pack walked with their heads held high, straight into the den sites of the new species. They called them two-legs because that was how the creatures moved.

"Some time later, a dog not of the Maisha pack emerged saying he heard thunder come from the two-legs den. The Maisha pack never left it. However, over the past few generations, every now and then, someone will spot one of the dogs from the Maisha pack, beckoning them to follow. It is believed that the Maisha pack protects us, even today. When we are threatened by the two-legs, the Maisha pack will lead us to safety. That's why we came here to Paradise. The Maisha pack led us here."

The pups stared at Yuri wide-eyed. "Wow! That's the best story ever, Dad!"

Yuri chuckled. "Wait until you meet Halili. She tells the best stories."

"Who's Halili?"

This question led to another story. I smiled to myself and laid my head on my paws, half-way listening to Yuri and pups. Life couldn't have been more perfect.

Chapter Fourteen: Fables

Spring came and went. The land flourished, as well as the animals in it. Rivers weaved through the land like snakes through grass. At the start of summer, the pups became restless. Their size made the den uncomfortably crowded. One evening, I heard them whispering well past bedtime from within the den. Yuri lay a short distance from me in quiet conversation with Kal. My soft chuckle grabbed his attention and he turned to me.

"What's so funny?" he asked, a smile lighting his face.

"I was just remembering the first time my brothers and I contemplated leaving the den. Sasha and Kanji had come up with the idea but they needed me to ask Mother. With all their courage, they still needed me."

"What made you think of that?"

"I think our little ones are having the same discussion. I can hear the dandelions spinning in their heads."

"It is getting close to time, isn't it?"

By this time, the rest of the pack tuned into our discussion. The pups leaving the den meant that we could move again. I think they were eager to stretch their legs.

"Yes," I answered for all their sakes. "It is nearly time."

A part of me feared leaving the den. While the predators in Paradise were limited, there was still a chance something could happen. I couldn't imagine how my mother raised so many pups without worrying all the time. Then again, maybe she did and just hid it well.

The next day, I told the pups they could sleep outside the den. Within a few days, we would leave it altogether. As expected, they were excited by the news. The rest of the pack shared in their enthusiasm before we set out for our morning hunt. Suri decided to stay with the pups while we were gone.

With the land beginning to dry out, the herds moved toward to the lake. This put us closer to the lions and we had to be extra vigilant while bringing down prey. As we neared the lake, however, we found little evidence of the lions presence. I found this odd and somewhat unsettling. Yuri understood my curious expression and shrugged his shoulders. I pushed the oddity behind me and focused on the hunt. That night, we heard the lions from far off. In fact, I almost didn't hear them at all.

"Where do you think they are?" I asked to no one in particular.

"It sounds like they are further north, near the other pride," answered Aahi. "Why would they be way up there? It isn't even their territory."

"Maybe something spooked them." Zephyr's comment left all of us speechless. What could spook a pride of lions? "Or maybe their king died and they are looking for another one."

The off-handed comment did not dispel our fears. We knew that a pride of lions, even one without a male, would not leave their home without provocation. And the only thing powerful enough to do that were two-legs.

"We're leaving tomorrow," I said as calmly as I could. Even I could hear the tremor in my voice.

"Mom, is everything alright?" Saki asked. She was the youngest of the pups and had a quiet demeanor, much like Marika.

"How about I tell you guys some riddles?" Kal said, capturing their attention.

"Wait a minute, Kal! That's my job," chided Soka.

"Calm down, little brother," he sighed. "I will keep all the cheesy ones for you."

The pups laughed at the brothers, releasing the tension of the moment.

"Okay, a giant turtle is traveling with a jackal, a rat, and a paw full of seeds. The turtle keeps everyone from eating each other with patience and wisdom. On their journey, they come to a wide river. None of them can cross it alone. Along the bank rests a small crocodile. The turtle, with all his wisdom, convinces the crocodile to allow them to cross the river on his back. The problem is, the crocodile is small and can only carry two things at a time. However, if the turtle leaves the jackal with the rat, it will eat it. And if he leaves the rat with the seeds, it will eat them. How does the turtle do it?"

The pups stared at each other trying to figure out the puzzle. Even Soka is stumped. After several minutes of quiet conversation, Toko spoke up.

"The turtle takes the rat across first and drops him off on the far bank. Then he goes back for the seeds. Once he drops off the seeds, he brings the rat back over and takes the jackal. With the jackal and the seeds on the far side, he goes back for the rat. It takes four trips but he does eventually get everyone across safely."

"Well, done!" Kal beamed. "Who knew you all were so smart. Here is another one. The Wind and the Sun argued about which was the stronger. One day, they noticed a pack of wild dogs curled around each other. The Sun said, 'I see a way to decide our dispute. Whichever of us can scatter that bundle of dogs shall be regarded as the stronger. You begin.' So the Sun retired behind a cloud, and the Wind began to blow as hard as it could upon the dogs hoping to push them apart by force. But the harder he blew the more closely the dogs bundled together, till at last the Wind had to give up in despair. Then the Sun came out and shone in all his glory upon the dogs. The heat from the sun warmed the dogs causing them to move apart."

The pups stared at Kal with vacant eyes. "Huh?" asked Toko. The moral was lost on the little ones and I burst out laughing. Kal cocked his head and sighed.

"Hold on, I got this," Soka said. "What animal can jump higher than a tree?"

"Well, that depends," answered Kali, my strategist. "Is it a small tree or a big tree? Does the tree bend when the wind blows? Is the animal standing above the tree, like on a mountain?"

"Grrrrrr! All animals jump higher than trees!" Soka cried. "Trees can't jump!"

Few a moment, everyone was quiet. Then, as one, we burst out laughing. I sometimes wondered if Soka were more like the pups than his brothers.

"All right, everyone," I called. "It's time to rest. We are moving out tomorrow and you are going to want to be rested when we do."

"Yes, Mother," the pups chorused. Surprisingly, they curled up between Soka and Kal. The brothers wrapped themselves around the growing pups and closed their eyes. Yuri moved closer to me and nudged my chin. I understood his meaning and leaned against him.

"Good night, mpendwa," he whispered.

"Good night."

The next day, we left the den, the pups following close behind us. We skirted the lake, looking for any recent signs of the lions. The herds did not seem agitated so I held out hope that the big cats were simply migrating for some reason. A few days into our travel, however, I came upon a familiar scent, one that left me trembling. The rest of the pack stopped and watched me curiously.

"What is it?" Yuri asked.

"Two-legs," Zephyr answered, her ears pointing straight ahead. "I smell them, too."

"Can you lead us safely away?" I asked. Zephyr had always been able to lead us out of danger.

"I think so. Follow me."

Walking on our toes, we followed her through the tall grasses. The scent of the two-legs slowly faded and by nightfall, was gone altogether. We rested that night on empty bellies. With the two-legs so near, it was dangerous to hunt. We would have to wait until the morning.

Following one of the main rivers, we headed north along Yuri's western border. A forest marked the border and sat at the base of the great mountain. In fact, almost the entire western border skirted the mountain. It was close to where I first met Halili and I wondered briefly if the elephants were still in the area.

Yuri, seeming to read my mind asked, "Would you like to take the pups to see Halili?"

"I think it would be a great time to take a break. Are they nearby?"

"Most likely. Halili likes to keep close to the watering hole on this side of Paradise while waiting for the rains to return. Other than our lake and the northern one, it is the largest body of water that survives the dry season. It's another day's travel or so."

"That sounds good to me. I know the pups could use the break and they will adore Halili."

The next day, we took a short detour to Halili's watering hole. We heard the trumpeting of the elephants before we saw them. The pups, having never seen or heard an elephant before nearly jumped out of their skins. I chuckled and led them through the trees hiding the small oasis. The rest of the pack rested in the shade of the trees.

"Hello, little M'vita," Halili trumpeted, her scratchy voice rumbling through the earth. "How has life been treating you?"

"Very well, thank-you. I have brought someone to see you."

Halili's ancient eyes lit up when I stepped aside, revealing the six enthralled puppies. They stared at her massive size in silent awe, their jaws dropping to their chest.

"Well, hello little ones," she said, lowering her head to the ground. "It is nice to meet you."

I pushed them toward her and they ran up to her resting form. I had told them stories about Halili but really, seeing is believing. I left them with her while I went to find my own rest. I knew they would be safe with her for a while.

"Once upon a time…" she began, slipping into her stories. The pups circled around her trunk, ears perked and attentive.

I returned to Yuri and the rest of the pack. The heat of the day and the exhaustive travel finally caught up to me. I stretched out under a tree and drifted off to sleep, Halili's deep voice my lullaby.

Chapter fifteen: Shattered

We rested at Halili's oasis the rest of the day and the following night. I checked on the pups at one point, only to find them sleeping against the elephant. Her ears flapped slowly, cooling both herself and the exhausted pups. Although her eyes were closed, I knew she was awake. A contented smile stretched across her face.

"What do we do now?" Yuri asked that evening once all the pups were asleep.

"I don't know," I answered, honestly. "If we stay in the south, we risk running into the two-legs but if we go north, we have to deal with the lions. Possibly two prides of them. Honestly, Yuri, the fact that the lions fled has me worried. If they were so afraid of the two-legs, then maybe we should be, too."

"I agree. We'll just have to keep a close eye out and try to stay away from the lions. Hopefully, the rains will drive the two-legs out and things can return to normal."

"Yeah, but the rains aren't due for several more weeks. I'll alert the pack tomorrow and come up with a plan."

The following morning, we said our goodbyes to Halili and the elephants and resumed our trek north. When we were far enough away from the oasis, we started our hunt. Being so close to the elephants, we held off hunting. That morning, we were ravenous. After filling our bellies, we found a cool place to rest.

The pups were off to the side playing lazily on their bellies.

I gathered the rest of the pack together to go over a plan. Marika kept a watchful eye out for the pups just in case. Kal, Yuri, and Soka moved close to me right while Aahi stayed near Marika as added support. Zephyr and Suri sat to my left.

Yuri, knowing the territory best, began. "The river that feeds Halili's oasis runs north along the western border, occasionally dipping into the forest beyond our borders. There is a stretch of parched earth before it swings back around, maybe a day's travel or so. If we follow it, I think we can avoid most trouble. There is plenty of hiding places. The hardest part is traveling through the arid stretch, especially with pups. We will have to travel through the day in the heat but once we get past it, everything should be fine."

We all nodded before he continued.

"Once we reach the northern section, there will be little water and the herds will have thinned. If we can make it to the north-eastern border, we will have plenty of food and water. A lake marks the line between our territory and my Mother's pack. I rarely travel that far north because it is so close to her but desperate times…Anyway, as long as we stay on our side, we should be fine. At least for a while."

"So, we just need to survive a few weeks of travel through some of the most hostile areas in our territory while dodging lions and fighting thirst and the heat with six young pups? Sounds easy enough to me." Soka's lighthearted tone did not ease the tension of the moment. This would be a tough journey and we all knew it.

Once the pups were rested, we set off. Following the river meant that we typically had food. The herds stayed close to the water. But I worried that every hunt would attract unwanted attention. Brave as they were, the pups began to show their exhaustion after the first week of constant travel. Soka and Marika pulled up the rear, making sure no one fell behind.

We reached the point where the river cut through the forest and decided to rest for the day. The pups, as well as the rest of the pack needed all the rest they could get before moving through the hardest part of the journey. Yuri told the pups to drink their fill and to rest. It was not a time for playing. His words didn't much matter. As soon as they had eaten and filled their bellies with water, they fell to sleep, a ball of fur and long legs.

The rest of the pack was subdued as well. Exhaustion claimed us all and we took the time to renew our energy.

That night, we once again heard the lions. They were close, much to close and their calls jolted me from my sleep. Somewhere off in the distance, another lion roared. It was the two prides. I may not have been a lion but I knew the two prides were much too close to one another.

Yuri woke as well and turned worried eyes to me. We would have to be even more vigilant. Tomorrow would be the hardest day the pups had ever known.

As though nature wanted to play a cruel trick, the following morning was the hottest of the season. The sun baked the earth and sent heat waves shimmering across the horizon, a sad mockery of water. I told the pups to drink well before starting our journey.

Heat, real, true heat, like that of an African summer, is something impossible to explain to someone who has never experienced it. Despite our need to move quickly, the heat sapped our strength. We moved with our feet barely lifted off the ground, a ground so hot, by the way, that it burned the sensitive pads of our feet. Our ears drooped and flopped with every careless bounce of our bodies. Panting was the only way to cool down but doing so left our mouths dry and cracked, our tongues lolling to the side.

The pups, as expected, took it especially hard. Around mid-day, they could no longer move. We found a bit of shade to sleep off the worst of the heat. Toko whimpered in his sleep and I worried over him.

When dusk came, we began to move again. By then, most of the heat had dissipated. Still, we could not locate the herds. Wild dogs rarely travel at night but given our desperate situation, we did on that one. For the first few hours after the sun set, we pushed through the night. The chilly night air eventually had us stopping and we curled up together to keep warm.

The lions were even closer that night. Even the pups were startled awake. We took turns staying awake to watch for danger. By morning, we were exhausted both from hunger, thirst, and lack of sleep. We pushed through the rest of the day, looking forward to once again finding the river.

It was nearing evening when we smelled the water. The pups, in their eagerness plunged ahead looking for the source. We all cried out as they sprinted ahead. But it was too late. We heard the roars of the lions just after the pups disappeared into the grass. Marika ran after them before we could stop her.

I don't even know how many lions there were. We tried to reach Marika and the pups but by the time we reached the rise they disappeared over, the lions were coming over it, roaring and swiping at us. We held our ground for as long as we could, growling and barking at the lionesses to move aside. But their empty eyes told me they had suffered their own losses and had no sympathy for mine.

We surrendered the ground, unable to save those who had been lost. When we were safely away, I called into the ground, hoping beyond hope that they had somehow managed to escape. I refused to believe that they were all gone. I spent hours calling to them until my voice was nearly gone.

Yuri, unable to listen anymore came up to me and pulled me against him.

"Shhh…" he whispered. "They aren't coming back, mpendwa."

"They have to," I cried, my voice hoarse. "They can't all be gone."

The rest of the pack surrounded us, grieving and whimpering.

"We have to keep moving," he said. "The lions aren't that far away and could come after us. I know it's hard, M'vita but we have to leave."

I swallowed the lump that formed in my throat and sucked in a deep breath. Yuri was right. The rest of the pack needed me to be strong. I would have plenty of time to grieve once we were safe.

"Let's go," I said with one last look behind me.

The rest of the pack followed behind without a sound. I had to remember that the grief was not mine alone. The pups were part of the pack, our future. Everyone grieved, the same as I. Yuri reminded me of Mother. He was strong because he had to be. Now I, too, would be strong when I had to be. I gained a greater understanding of my mother's sacrifice and why she did the things she did. Why she sometimes seemed so cold. It wasn't because she didn't care. It was evidence of her strength. I hoped that one day, I would be as strong as her.

It took several more days to reach the northeastern borders. All along the way we heard the lions roaring to each other. It was no wonder they attacked us. For all they knew, we were the rival pride or some other predator coming to do them harm. Despite my grief, I didn't hate the lions. They did not attack us out of hate or anger.

The land that Yuri spoke of was as beautiful as I'd imagined, nearly as beautiful as the southern floodplain. If not for the lions, it might have been perfect. I found myself wishing the pups and Marika had been able to see it.

The rains came on time, flooding the land as it did every year. I realized another reason Yuri did not choose this place to live. Unlike the southern floodplain, which had high ground to escape to, the northern lake did not. When the rains came, the entire area flooded and we found ourselves trying to outrun it. Hoping beyond hope that the heavy rains pushed out the two-legs, we made our way south. It was time to return home.

Chapter Sixteen: Alone

We avoided the old den sites as we made our way south. Not only did I not want to be reminded of what I lost, the rains collapsed most of them. As it was, we had no need of them anyway. We marked our territorial lines as we traveled. Although we had not seen any evidence of other dogs, instinct told us to reestablish them, just in case.

Paradise is uniquely situated in a way that territorial boundaries are easy to maintain. Nestled into a large bowl that stretches farther than one can see, it is bordered on the south and east by a high ridge that overlooks the area. It was here my sisters and I first came to Paradise. The western border is a vast forest and the single gigantic mountain, almost as if the behemoth guarded the whole place. The forest stretches around the northern border, the only break in the dense trees being the northern lake. Given its unique geography, establishing territorial lines was simple. Our borders were hard to miss.

We braved the rains everyday as we traveled home, skirting the higher ground of the eastern border. Being so high up offered me a different perspective of the land I called home, and a greater respect for its sheer size. Over the weeks of travel, the worst of the grief faded. Survival meant that we had to push on and heal quickly. I think the losses from my childhood also helped to prepare me. By the time we returned to the southern floodplain, most of the pain and emptiness I had felt faded.

The worst of the rains abated when we finally reached home. The time of rebirth had come and the animals, predator and prey alike basked in its glory. For the first time in weeks, a genuine smile found our faces.

"Welcome home, mpendwa," Yuri said, looking out across his territory.

"Welcome home," I answered back.

The following weeks we traversed the soaked land as we had the spring before, minus one dog. Hunting proved plentiful and we began to really enjoy ourselves again. I watched as the herds doubled in size. At one point, even Halili and her herd came down to the lake. The elephants looked happy and healthy. They were too far away for us to go and say hello so we just watched them from the rise where we were resting.

The southern lion pride also returned. To my surprise, the old male who led it my first season in Paradise still led the pride. I had imagined the worst when the two prides were in such close proximity. In truth, I did not know which pride was responsible for the losses to our pack but I was glad to see this pride back to its usual selves. It meant they would not needlessly trouble us, if we kept our distance.

As spring carried on, I knew a difficult and important discussion would soon be coming. Not one to disappoint, Yuri approached me a few weeks after the herds began their birthing cycle.

"M'vita, can we speak for a moment?" he asked.

The rest of the pack looked at us curiously. I nodded my head and he led me a short distance away from the others, far enough away so that they could not overhear.

"I know this is difficult but…" he began, stumbling over his words.

"I know what you are going to ask," I said, rescuing him any embarrassment. "I agree that it is time to try again."

A smile lit up his face and he nuzzled against me. My heart squeezed for a second before I returned his affection. In life, we live and learn. When tragedy strikes, the best one can do is dust themselves off and learn from it. The loss of my first litter could not stop me from having others. I knew I would have losses. The best I could do was learn from them. Unfortunately, some losses prove to be too much to handle.

When we made our trek north the last summer, we managed to avoid the two-legs that had invaded our home. In fact, looking back, we did not see any evidence of them for some time before reaching Halili's oasis. When the rains came, they erased whatever evidence remained. The fact that there was no evidence had us almost forgetting the danger. After all, we only left because the lions did.

As spring progressed and the land flourished, the threat of the two-legs became a distant memory. The herds moved across the floodplain, oblivious to any danger, except for that of the few predators that dotted the landscape. The lions welcomed a new litter into the world and we were preparing for our own.

The second worse day of my life started like any other. Late spring brought with it an abundance of life. The land rolled away from us in undulating waves of brilliant green grasses and colorful wildflowers. The waters had tamed somewhat, limiting themselves to a multitude of rivers, streams, and ponds. Animals welcomed the morning with glory, the grazers sending out puffs of mist as they snorted and swung their heads side to side.

That morning dawned bright without a single cloud to mar its beauty. I woke feeling refreshed and stretched out my muscles. We had eaten the night before so I wasn't all that hungry. The rest of the pack followed suit, waking one by one.

"What would you like to do today?" Yuri asked to no one in particular.

"I think we should move around the southern border," Kal answered. "The rains kept us from marking that border and today seems like the perfect day for a run."

"I like that idea," I said, nodding my approval.

As soon as the sun burned off the morning mist, we moved toward the southern border. This led us around the lake with a high ridge to our left. On the lower ground, the lake nearly disappeared at times from our field of vision. It sat quite a distance away. The herds kept closer to the floodplain where the grass was greenest. With the exception of a few flocks of birds flying overhead, a peaceful quiet followed us on our journey. We didn't speak and just enjoyed the silence.

The entire southern border would take several days to traverse. By mid-day, we had barely made it around the bend. A small herd of gazelle had wandered too far south, giving us the perfect opportunity to hunt. After feeding, we stretched out in the shade of a giant acacia tree, taking a moment to rest.

I drifted in and out of consciousness, the vibrations from the earth lulling me into a near-sleep. In my semi-conscious state, I didn't at first realize that the vibrations were unnatural. You see, the earth, air, water, everything in life gives off vibrations. It is how our energy manifests. So, the fact that the earth vibrated wasn't something foreign to me. What was foreign, was the fact that the vibrations slowly increased. Unless there is a storm, the vibrations within the earth are always steady. That day, there wasn't a cloud in the sky.

By the time I took note of the oddity, the earth rubbled through my chest and belly. My mind fought against my lethargy, demanding me to wake, telling me that the sensation was an all-too familiar one. My memories jolted me awake and I jumped to my feet before my eyes had even fully cleared.

"Everyone, get up!" I cried, scanning the area for the source of the rumbling.

The pack jumped to their feet, just then taking notice of what I already had.

"M'vita, is that...?" Suri asked, her ears swiveling around.

"Two-legs," I answered her unfinished question. "We have to hide."

But it was too late. The two-legs' contraptions, two of them, flew over a dip in the land we hadn't even noticed. As soon as we turned to run, they spotted us. The ridge at our backs limited our options for escape and the two-legs came right at us. In the end, we split up. Suri, Soka, and Zephyr headed west toward an outcropping of rocks, hoping to hide within them. Me, Yuri, Kal, and Aahi turned northeast toward the lake. I had a den that I secretly hoped hadn't collapsed after the rains.

The two-legs turned their contraptions to follow us, one going east and one going west. Despite the wind in my ears, I still heard Suri yelp and the others growling at the two-legs. I couldn't stop to see what was happening so I just plunged ahead. I turned worried eyes to Yuri.

"Don't look back," he said. "Just keep going. We're almost there."

The two-legs were fast. Their contraption fell on us just as we reached the den. Only one dog could fit in at a time and the brothers made way for me. Just as I slipped into the darkness, I heard Aahi yelp. Yuri turned toward the two-legs, growling and snarling.

"Yuri!" I cried. "You can't fight them. Get in here!"

At first, Yuri didn't answer. All I could hear was growling from the three brothers. I started to crawl back out but Yuri snapped at the entrance.

"Don't come out!" he said. "They can't get you in there."

"Yuri, please!"

He shot me one last look, full of desperation and sadness, and then he was gone. A single yelp told me the two-legs had won. My stomach twisted.

When I felt the earth rumble again, I moved out of the den. I could see the brothers locked in the thorn bushes on the back of the human contraption as it moved away from me. Yuri barked, telling me to stay hidden. I stared until the two-legs disappeared from sight.

What about the others? I thought. *Surely the two-legs didn't take everyone.* I made my way toward the rocks where the others had gone, my legs stretching as far as they could. I barked, calling to what remained of my pack but no call answered me. When I reached the outcropping, I realized the others had never made it. I was completely and utterly alone in a land without a single wild dog, save me.

Chapter Seventeen: Adaptations

Wild dogs were never meant to live alone. That's why we have packs. In Paradise, it was even worse. Not only had I lost my pack, my family, the odds were bleak on me ever finding another. Unless other dogs braved the journey through the forest or over the ridge and had the courage to cross Yuri's boundary, the chances of finding another pack were near impossible.

Unless I leave, I thought, the idea a punch in the gut. Where would I go? Even if I left and found another pack, would they accept me?

I wandered for days with no clear destination. My mind fell into a fog with only three things repeating themselves: eat, sleep, and move. Of course, as a single dog, my hunting options were limited. I couldn't bring down big prey. I couldn't even catch the young herd animals that had be born that year. I found myself sniffing out rodents and reptiles, anything that couldn't outrun me.

One morning, maybe two weeks or so after my pack had been taken, I finally broke free of my daze. Something else needed me and in that moment, I found purpose once again.

As I lay resting with my eyes closed and ears perked, I heard the soft whimpering of a small animal, almost like that of a wild dog pup. Curious, I lifted my head and turned it, trying to locate the sound. A small clump of rocks beckoned me and I approached. As I reached it, a tiny nose peaked out.

I couldn't see into the darkness so I wasn't entirely sure what I was looking at. I stepped back just a little and called for the creature.

"Come on out, little one," I soothed. "You are safe."

"Where is Mother?" it squeaked. "She has been gone for days. Father, too."

I gathered something had orphaned the creatures. But what could I do? I still didn't even know what they were.

"I don't know," I answered. "But I can watch over you until they come back. You must be hungry, if it has been days since your parents came home."

After a few minutes of silence, two tiny pups emerged. They weren't wild dog pups, as I had suspected. After a minute of searching my memory, I realized they were jackal pups, too old to be still nursing but too young to survive on their own. They pulled their ears back, their whole bodies shaking.

"Hi there," I said. "You are safe now. I won't let anything happen to you."

The pups ran to me, licking my jaw. In reflex, I regurgitated my meager meal from that morning. In a strange twist of fate, I found myself a new pack.

Over the next few months, the jackals and I stayed together. They grew quickly and proved effective hunters. While I still couldn't bring down large prey, we were able to eat well and, on occasion, take down a small antelope. We stayed together all summer and well into the rainy season. Together, we traversed Yuri's territory. Well, I suppose at that point, it was my territory. I taught the pups everything I knew, how to hunt, how to mark one's territory, what dangers to look out for.

Ironically, the lions paid us no mind at all. We could be sitting several feet away from them and they acted as if we weren't even there. I guess they figured the jackals weren't a threat and didn't want to waste energy chasing them off. When spring came, we went our separate ways. At least for a little while.

Nuru, the female cub, returned after several weeks. She was not alone. She had found a mate, Zuberi, and brought him back to her "pack". That was a day that will stay with me for as long as I live.

Unlike Nuru, Zuberi grew up with his parents. He was taught the ways of the jackal by other jackals whereas Nuru grew up more like a wild dog. While some things are the same, such as the fact that both species mate for life, some are drastically different. One main difference, and the one that caused the most dissension, was that jackals, unlike wild dogs, do not live in packs. They survive as a mated pair alone.

In the end, Zuberi and I came to an agreement. We could still hunt and travel together, but I had to give the family space. I could not rest too near the den site. I think part of it was the fact that Nuru was expecting pups and Zuberi did not want them learning the ways of the wild dog. Over time, he began to accept me as part of Nuru's life. It wasn't ideal, but it was enough for me.

The following spring, I added another wayward character to my ragtag pack. A young hyena found herself separated from her pack. I think the lions scattered them about and little Aki was lost in the confusion. In truth, it was never my intention to adopt a hyena. Hyenas are dangerous and have been know to kill wild dogs and jackals. We actually ran from them quite often in my youth.

But when I found the youngling, she was whimpering and shivering. It didn't take much coaxing to get her to follow me. I only planned to help her find her missing pack but the spotted pup attached herself to me and refused to leave. After a week of searching, she was reunited with her pack. To my disbelief, however, she did not stay with them. Instead, she traveled back and forth, even hunting with us.

Getting Zuberi to accept Aki was harder than getting him to accept me. He was livid the first time Aki tried to hunt with us, even refusing to leave the den site. But, I explained that, with Aki, we could take down bigger prey. Eventually, he agreed. That night, we had more than enough to eat.

Another positive thing came from Aki joining our pack. The hyena hierarchy is such that females are revered and respected. Despite Aki's young age, this same principle held true for her. The hyena pack respected her and, in turn, those she held dear, to include me and the jackals. They formed a sort of extended pack. I couldn't go into the hyena pack but they wouldn't needlessly cause me any trouble, either.

When Nuru and Zuberi's pups came, the alliance made them more protected than any other jackal pups in all of Paradise.

As time does, it passed in stages. Spring came and went, bringing generations of new life to the floodplains. Although I had the whole of Paradise to myself, I limited my territory to the southern floodplain where my new family spent their time. They had no need to travel so far north so neither did I.

Summer drifted by, bringing with it bounty, warm evenings, and brilliant sunsets. The animals in Paradise flourished, from the herds, the predators big and small, to the countless species of birds that migrated to and fro. I watch as the land healed. Even the elephants were regaining their strength. I watched as the two-legs brought in a handful of gigantic males to help boost the population. I laughed to myself, wondering what Halili would think of that.

When the land started to wilt from the heat and the waters ran dry, I watched as the rains returned, drenching the world once again. Sometimes, when it was especially quiet or I found myself alone, I closed my eyes and focused everything on the energy flowing through me. It took age and wisdom to understand how my mother lived for as long as she did while staying strong.

As I felt the energy, I realized that all those I had lost, aunts, uncles, sisters, brothers…my children. They never really left. They surrounded me with their energy every day, filling me with their strength. Sometimes, I even imagined I could hear them, laughing and playing. These moments filled me with contentment. I probably should have been sad after losing so much. But I wasn't. My life was full of happiness.

Two summers passed with my new pack. I helped raise two litters of jackal pups. Even Aki had a litter, although I wasn't able to approach them. Like wild dogs, hyenas raise their pups together, as a pack. I was okay with that. I listened as Aki told me stories of their antics.

Nuru and Zuberi started to spend more time alone during that third year. Maybe it was age, I'm not sure. But they became more independent. We would occasionally still hunt together but more often than not, I would stay at the den and babysit while they went out alone. This was actually the only time I could play with the pups. Zuberi forbid me get too close when he was around.

Near the end of summer, just after the pups were weaned, I felt the distant rumblings of the two-legs. The vibrations were barely noticeable and if I hadn't already been awake, I probably wouldn't even have noticed. The direction signaled that it was most likely the same two-legs who came occasionally to bring new animals into Paradise. With the pups asleep and safely ensconced within their den, I made my way to the ridge.

I traveled quite some time before cresting it. Luckily, the two-legs' contraption was still moving. I spied the dust trail marking their movement and followed it until it stopped. For several minutes, nothing happened. They were too far away to see anything clearly and I strained my eyes against the sun.

All of a sudden, two large forms shot into the brush, followed closely by two more, their spotted bodies disappearing before I could even identify what they were. Although they were similar to leopards, their sleek bodies suggested something else.

Cheetahs! I thought. I had never actually seen a cheetah in my youth and there were none in Paradise. A new predator had come to Paradise, something that had been missing for far too long.

Chapter Eighteen: New Arrivals

The return of the cheetah had an interesting effect on the animals of Paradise. All of the grazers, with the exception of the oldest elephants, had been born after the cheetahs disappeared. In fact, several generations had born and died since then. Because of this, the herds did not know what to make of the fleet-footed felines. Having experience with lions and leopards, the herds knew the cheetahs were dangerous. However, unlike lions and leopards, who usually hunted at dusk or at night, the cheetahs hunted during the heat of the day.

The speed at which the cats moved also surprised the herds. In truth, I had never seen anything move so fast, although sometimes, the gazelle were quite fleet-footed themselves. It amazed me to watch the cheetahs hunt. I was always raised to believe the only cats who lived as a pack were lions. But the way the cheetahs worked together, they looked very much like a pack to me.

Although there were four cheetahs the first day they arrived, I only ever saw three after that. I guessed something must have happened to the fourth one, possibly a predator or maybe the two-legs, even though I hadn't seen the two-legged hunters in quite some time.

Of the three that remained, one looked different than the others. Where the other two were spotted, this one had black patches with stripes down its back and tail. It was also considerably larger and had longer fur. I admit being intrigued. Was he their leader? I would watch them for hours from the safety of the den site. The more I watched them, however, it didn't seem like they had a leader at all.

Just after the cheetahs came to Paradise, the rains returned. For some reason, this year I found myself wishing for home. Perhaps it was the cheetahs that brought on my melancholy. Thoughts of my brothers and sisters and Yuri and our pack filled my lonely nights. Zuberi and Nuru spent almost the entire rainy season ensconced in their den and Aki moved with the hyenas. The lions left the floodplain to patrol their borders and the hyenas followed. I knew I would need to patrol mine as well but I just couldn't muster up enough energy to move.

Near the end of the rainy season, I decided to go see Halili. The elephant's wisdom could help me overcome my loneliness and I hadn't see her since just before the pups had died.

I traveled through the heart of my territory, the quickest and most straightforward route. Occasionally, I would see the herds on the move.

The cheetahs settled into my home nicely. Halili and her herd gathered around the old matriarch as she addressed them. I didn't mean to eavesdrop but, well…the elephants are quite enormous and I do have large ears.

They decided to leave the oasis, at least for a time, and explore Paradise in its splendor. With the new males in the area, it would also make it possible for a new generation to join the herd. I chuckled to myself. At least she wasn't completely against the new additions. If I didn't know better, I would think she even fancied one of them.

They broke formation and started to move out. I had only ever seen Halili up close while she rested on her belly. I have to admit that seeing her standing, in all her glory was intimidating.

"Halili," I called, my voice drowned out by the noise of a large herd of elephants.

Luckily, Halili had large ears, too and heard me over the ruckus. She turned her head to me and smiled. "Well, hello little one. It has been too long."

"I apologize for that," I said, looking down for a moment. "I lot has happened."

I followed alongside the elephants for the rest of the day. After telling Halili all that had happened, I listened to what she had to say. She talked for hours in her deep, soothing voice. Sometimes she gave me her wisdom on what I should do now. But mostly, she just told stories, all kinds of stories. It reminded me a little of Soka and his riddles and I found myself laughing more than I thought possible.

By the end of the day, my melancholy had disappeared and I felt renewed, ironic given that it was the beginning of spring. I bid Halili and the elephants a fond farewell and turned my white-tufted tail for home.

That spring, Aki joined the hyena ranks for good. The elderly matriarch, her mother, passed from our world and Aki took up the mantle of leadership. At first, I missed her company. Aki was an interesting character, as were the hyenas in general. I never thought I would understand the slope-backed animals so well when I was just a pup, afraid of my own shadow.

Overall, though, I was happy for her. It was a great honor in hyena society to lead a pack and the others looked up to her. Watching her, I knew she would be a great leader.

Although Nuru and Zuberi still tolerated my presence, they rarely spent any time with me, other than hunting. I found myself walking my territory alone quite often. One thought kept filling my mind during my walks: should I leave Paradise?

Nuru had her pups late in the season, at the beginning of summer. Normally, this could have meant trouble. Food and water grow scarce and the parents have to travel further from the den to find it. However, with me as babysitter, the pups were safe, even if Nuru and Zuberi were gone most of the day.

At first, I hunted with Zuberi while Nuru stayed with the pups. We had formed a strange bond over the years so the companionship wasn't uncomfortable. One day, just before Nuru weaned the pups, Zuberi struck up a conversation with me. This was strange because Zuberi typically preferred silence.

"I want to thank you for what you have done for my family, M'vita," he said. "I know you have given up a lot, including having one of your own."

"It wasn't any trouble, Zuberi," I told him. "It is your family that has kept me from succumbing to loneliness. I can't imagine where I would be, if not for you."

"Why don't you just leave? Find other wild dogs?"

"This is my home. All of my most precious memories are here. And who's to say the others won't come back someday."

He nodded and we continued the rest of the hunt in silence. I do not know if he fully understood what I was saying but I think he gained a little more respect for me.

That summer proved to be one of the hottest I can ever remember in Paradise. Much of the land dried out, including a good portion of the southern floodplain. Nuru had to move her den closer to the lake but far enough away to not be in the path of the migrating herds. Unfortunately, that put us in close proximity to other predators. The pups were old enough to explore the area around the den site which meant someone had to keep a watchful eye on them at all times. More often than not, this was me.

"Listen up, you little monsters," I said, endearingly. "I'm going to go just over there to get some water. Can I trust you to stay here and be quiet for a few minutes?"

"Yes, auntie 'vita," the three pups chorused.

It didn't take long to quench my thirst but it was long enough for danger to find the pups. The cheetahs had been like ghost all summer. I rarely saw any evidence of them even being in Paradise and, to be honest, had almost forgotten all about them. As I approached the den, however, movement from the corner of my eye caught me attention.

I told the pups to play quietly and that their parents were on their way. Then I moved a little away and laid on my belly in the shade. Whatever was in the shadows did not move so I continued as if everything was fine. No need to start trouble if the creature were simply hiding.

A moment later, Zuberi and Nuru reached the den, regurgitating the pups' meal. When they were fully engaged in eating, I turned to the animal that still hid. I wanted to lead it away from the den site so I stood and started to walk away, turning back to beckon it to follow me. Without alerting the jackals, a cheetah slipped quietly from the grass and began to follow.

We walked until sunset, far enough away from the den for the cheetah to get the point that I did not want her there. When I was confident she understood what I wanted, I stopped and lay down in the grass. The heat from the day was already starting to dissipate. She stretched out her long legs next to me. I could tell she was just as lonely as me.

"I have never seen your kind here before but I have heard stories from long ago," I began, turning to her. "Truthfully, I'm surprised you have returned."

"Why?" she asked, seemingly surprised by my words.

"Because it is not safe for you here."

I thought back to her unique brother. Although the two-legs had not returned for some time, I knew her brother would be a much sought-after prize when they did. Her shocked expression showed her inexperience.

"Why do you say that?" she asked.

"The cheetah didn't just disappear. They were killed, some by lions. But most were killed by the hunters who walk on two legs. Not just the cheetah, but most of the animals in this paradise."

"But, there are countless animals here."

I knew she doubted my motives. It was time she heard the truth and I doubted Halili would welcome a cheetah into her herd.

"It was a long time ago, before I was even born. And I have seen many turns of the seasons. Would you like to hear the story from the beginning?"

"Yes," she answered, as eager as I was when I first heard the stories of Paradise.

I spent most of the evening telling the cheetah the stories Halili told me. I started at the beginning, when Paradise flourished with all kinds of plants and animals. Then I told her about the two-legs and their war and the subsequent fall of Paradise. Lastly, I told her how Paradise began to recover, sometimes with the help of other two-legs. She listened with rapt attention. I finished with my own tale.

"Unfortunately, no wild dogs have returned and I am the last of my family," I finished

"I am very sorry for your loss," she said with sympathy. "It must be very lonely. Back home, we often observed wild dog packs. There were too many to count."

"I am finding my place," I said honestly with only a hint of sadness. "My adopted family has given me much joy and I have made other unlikely friends."

"If the land is recovering, why do you fear for my brothers and I?"

"The hunters did not stay gone. Sometimes, deep in the night, they slip back in and kill certain animals, mostly the elephants and big cats. Your spotted coat is a prize to them. And I have seen your unique brother once. He is especially in danger. If the hunters see him, they will stop at nothing to possess his pelt."

"That's terrible!"

"It is worse for the elephants. Some of the old matriarchs were alive when the hunters first came. They remember the reign of terror that followed and watched in horror as many of their kin were slaughtered for their tusks."

We sat quietly for the next few minutes. She needed time to process all that I had said. Given that she had been in Paradise a year already, I doubted she and her brothers would leave. This land had a way of holding onto you, making it to where you never wanted to leave.

"If I can give you some advice," I continued, breaking the silence. "Keep to the middle of the land, near the lake or close to the forest where you can quickly hide. The lions frequent there but the hunters do not like to travel too deeply into our territory. And the hunters are much more dangerous than the lions."

"Thank-you…uh…"

"M'vita. And you're welcome. I really hope to see you again and maybe even young ones one day."

"Thanks, M'vita. I'm Sahara. And I hope for the same for you."

We got to our feet and headed our separate ways. I turned back once to watch her disappear over a rise. A smile stretched across my face. No one would ever believe that I had made friends with a cheetah!

Chapter Nineteen: Hunters

Another rainy season came and went. Not only was the prior summer hotter and longer than usual, the rainy season was shorter. It seemed ominous but the energy I always felt at this time poured into me, same as always so I let the feeling pass. Nuru's pups were nearly old enough to leave but, unlike the others, decided to stay and help with the next litter.

Perhaps it was because Nuru and Zuberi were getting older.

Whatever the reason, it left no room for me. I bid my adopted family goodbye and headed north. It was time to patrol my territory anyway and I hadn't been to the northern border in a long time.

It took several weeks to skirt around the eastern border and reach the northern floodplain. Beautiful as ever, I took a moment to appreciate my home. I sat on a cliff overlooking miles of land all around me. I could almost see over the tops of the trees that marked the northern border. For a moment, I wondered if Yuri's birth pack still patrolled that land.

A few days later, I made my way to the west. Ever vigilant of the northern lion pack, the silence of the night left me curious. Where were they? I traveled all the way to the forest of the western border without a single sign of any lions. As I made my way south, closer to Halili's oasis, I finally found a carcass that showed evidence of lions. They were heading toward the southern floodplain.

My mind flashed with memories of the last time that happened. Two-legged hunters had come from the south, chasing the southern lions north. I scanned the area for the two-legs but I was on low ground and out in the open. I would never see them where I was.

Without intending to, I thought about Sahara. If the two-legs were here, the cheetahs were in danger. Remembering that she and her brothers typically stayed south of the southern floodplain, I relaxed. I had time to warn them if I didn't encounter any of the lions on the way.

Several days into my journey, I heard short cracks of thunder off to the northeast. The rains had ended months ago and I turned my head to find a clear blue sky. Not a cloud in sight. I search my memory for anything that could make that sound but came up empty. Shrugging my shoulders, I continued south. I needed to reach the cheetahs before the hunters did.

Along the way, I stopped at Halili's oasis to warn her of the hunters. She had a flock of birds that called her oasis home and she asked them to warn the other elephants of the danger. That spring, a small herd of younger elephants had branched off to form their own herd. By that time, they were clear across Paradise, probably headed either south to the southern floodplain or northeast to the northern one. Truthfully, I was surprised I did not see them on their journey.

After leaving Halili's home, I beelined it to the south. I had to skirt around the northern lion pride as they ate. The last thing I needed was to get in a skirmish with them. Toward the end of summer, I finally reached the place Sahara and her brothers usually stayed, only to find it occupied by the southern lion pride. Which meant the cheetahs were somewhere else.

"I hope you're safe, Sahara," I said to myself. I did all I could. With nothing else to do, I headed back toward the jackal's den. I may not be of any help but being near them would keep me from getting lonely, even if I only observed from afar.

Change came with that summer. The two lion prides collided often. The southern pride refused to give the northern one sanctuary. I imagine it had been the same when the southern pride had to flee their home. But, the northern pride was resilient and they had greater numbers, including two males that ruled the pride. The greatest advantage to the interlopers, however, was their experience.

The north is a harsher place and the lions had to adapt to tougher situations. They were bigger and stronger and living through tougher times made them more than happy to take the land from their southern neighbors. This seemingly small change affected everyone from the elephants all the way down to the field mice. The northern lions did not respect the land of the south the way the southern lions did. All they saw was abundance for the taking.

I stayed near the jackals as an extra set of eyes, just in case. Unfortunately, there wasn't much I could do about Aki and her hyenas. But Aki was strong and brave. I didn't really need to worry about her.

Probably the biggest change came near the end of summer. While patrolling the eastern border, nearest the jackals, I stumbled across a vaguely familiar scent. Although it had been years since I smelled another wild dog, I was certain the scent belonged to them. That night, I camped near the border. Far off, almost too far to hear, I was sure I heard a pack barking. I did not hear them again nor find their scent but it did put a spark of hope in my heart.

The hunters never came to the southern floodplain but I would occasionally hear the strange cloudless thunder. When the rainy season began, we all breathed a deep sigh of relief. The northern lions returned home, bringing peace back to the southern floodplain.

A few weeks into the rainy season, as I patrolled my territory, I ran across a familiar scent. I chuckled to myself and followed it to a large rock heated by the sun. Sahara lounged across it, her long legs stretched out to take advantage of every ray of sunshine. I huffed to get her attention.

"I'm glad to see that you are still alive," I said when she turned her golden eyes on me. "But you are alone. How are your brothers?"

I realized too late that not all of the cheetahs had survived the hunters. Before I could say anything, she answered.

"N'dugu is well but we lost Soji to the hunters."

I wracked my brain for a minute trying to remember which one of her brothers was Soji. Was it the one with the unique fur pattern? "I'm sorry for your loss," I said. I didn't want to ask her which brother it was.

"How have you been?" she asked, changing the subject.

"Content. The little ones are off finding families of their own so it is a little lonely right now. However..." I thought back to the dogs that may or may not be in

Paradise. The rains had washed away any trace of them.

"What it is?" she asked, pulling me back into the conversation.

"I think there may be a pack of dogs nearby."

She jumped up and leapt from the rock. The sudden movement jumpstarted my instinct to flee and I jumped back.

"Sorry," she said, sheepish. "Have you seen them?"

"Not yet, but I can smell their scent and sometimes I hear them."

"That's great! Are you going to try to find them?"

"I don't know. I have been on my own for so long it feels kind of strange being among my own kind again. And what if they don't accept me?"

"This could be your only chance to find others like you. I think you should go for it."

"Maybe you're right. Good luck, Sahara. Remember to watch your back. If the wild dogs are returning, maybe the cheetah will, too."

"Thanks, and good luck to you, too."

With a nod, I turned and trotted off.

In any case, it was time for me to figure out where I belonged. The jackals no longer needed me. Aki was well on her way to ruling her own kingdom. And life was returning to Paradise. The young elephant herd that branched off from Halili's group trumpeted out by the lake. They decided to stay close to home for now and that was alright by me.

As spring progressed, I decided to once again patrol my land. Maybe I could find the elusive pack of wild dogs hidden away somewhere I hadn't been to in a while. I started off at the southern border where most of the waters had settled. Sure, I probably should have headed north first but I really wanted to go see Halili and the northern route would take months.

In a couple of weeks, I reached Halili's oasis. A large number of calves had been born that year and they all sat around her as she told stories. I sat back in the shadows and listened for a long time before anyone noticed me. Halili, seemingly oblivious to my presence, shooed the little ones off to go play in the cool water.

"If you keep coming around so often, I may have to adopt you into my herd," she said, turning to me.

"I should have known you'd noticed me," I chuckled, coming out from the bushes. "And for the record, I wouldn't mind being adopted by you."

"Have you heard them?"

"Them?" I asked, pretending not to know what she was talking about.

"The wild dogs. I hear them sometimes, off to the north, almost to the tree line. Have you not patrolled your northern border yet?"

I shrugged sheepishly. "I wanted to come see you first."

"Are you not excited to be with others of your kind? You have been alone for so long."

I laid next to her on my belly and watched the elephants play and splash around. "I'm never really alone. But…the pack sparks a bit of fear in me. Rogue wild dogs are killed by rival packs. What if they don't accept me? What if they see me as a threat, especially given that this is my territory?"

"And what if they do accept you? Life is all about risk, M'vita. You have lived here many turns of the seasons and have been mostly alone for almost all of them. You have to ask yourself, are you content to live out the rest of your days as you have been or would you rather risk the chance to spend them surrounded by your own kind?"

I contemplated what she had said a while before answering. "As always, your wisdom has put things in perspective, Halili. Thank-you for always sharing you guidance with me."

"Think nothing of it, dear. We are all here to help each other. It is the only way we can all survive and thrive and Paradise is well on its way to thriving."

I bid her farewell and headed off toward the east. I wasn't quite ready to head north just yet but I would follow her advice. I would follow the eastern border along the ridge and if the dogs were there, I would decide then whether or not to approach them.

Chapter Twenty: My Home

Another spring passed into summer as I made my way back across my territory. I took my time, in no big hurry to be anywhere. As I traveled, I took in my world. I didn't really notice before Halili mentioned it, but I started to feel my age. It wasn't really a bad feeling, just a little tightening in my muscles that wasn't there before and I spent more time resting than I did running around.

I took in everything as though with new eyes.
Early summer was probably my favorite time of year.
Sure, spring renewed the earth with life, water, and
green grasses dotted with a multitude of tiny, colorful
flowers. But with summer came a kind of order, if
order can ever be found in nature. The lakes and
rivers returned to their proper banks. Young born in
the spring began to take on adult characteristics.
And the sky filled with countless flocks of birds
traveling this way and that.

In all my years in Paradise, the animals, predator
and prey alike grew to know me as the only wild dog
in the land. This made me a little famous and the
animals respected me. I never took more than I
needed and I befriended all sorts of creatures.
Some, like Zuberi, held a grudging respect for me. I
was an old matriarch, much like Halili and without
realizing it, I facilitated a type of peace. Perhaps this
happened after I sent the warning about the hunters.
All I know is that as I traveled over the land, animals

would stop and watch me pass, often nodding their heads in my direction.

At that point, as I stood in the very center of Paradise, I realized I didn't need a pack to feel complete. I had everything a dog could ever want all around me. I smiled, a warmth filling my heart. With nowhere particular to go, I trotted off toward the lake. If there were wild dogs in Paradise, they could have the northern territory. I no longer had need of it.

One afternoon, during the hottest summer to date, I lounged under an acacia tree near the eastern border. I'm not sure what it was about that border but I always seemed to gravitate toward it. The cicadas were especially loud and all I wanted to do was borrow into the ground to get away from them. For some reason, my tree attracted every one in the area.

I sighed and flicked my ear in annoyance. "Can you quiet it down just a little?" I asked uselessly. "It's bad enough I'm baking in the heat. Go find another tree."

Of course, they didn't listen to me. Probably didn't even understand what I was saying. I pulled my paws over my ears hoping to block out some of the sound. I did help, a little. A rumbling in the rock had me lifting my head and turning toward the ridge, the cicadas forgotten. Of course, the insects didn't act as if anything was out of the ordinary. They continued on with their mating calls as though everything was normal.

I knew better. I'd felt those vibrations before, that unnatural energy that permeated the air like an intruder. I watched as a two-legged's contraption crested the hill. It moved at a reckless pace, bouncing from one foot to the other. Just after disappearing over the ridge, another came up behind it. Unlike the first one, however, this one stopped.

I froze. Resting under the tree as I was, the two-legs could easily see me. Even if I ran, there was nowhere to hide. Two two-legs fell from the contraption. Even with my limited experience with them, instinct told me these two-legs were not dangerous. Still, I had no desire to get near them.

One of them, an ebon-skinned male with fur the color of grass held up a stick. I heard a soft whoosh sound and felt a sting in my hip. As the two-legs lowered the stick, my head began to feel fuzzy. I watched as they approached but for some reason, my legs refused to move. In a matter of seconds, I drifted off to oblivion.

Before darkness completely claimed me, however, a vaguely familiar pale two-legs with golden hair whispered, "Shh…C'est bon, un peu." Of course, I didn't understand what he said but it left me feeling safe and protected.

When I awoke, the two-legs were gone, all evidence of their being there gone with them. I lay under the same tree with the cicadas screaming as they were before I fell asleep. In truth, I was surprised I could sleep with all the noise they were making. A pounding radiated from the center of my head and my mouth felt as dry as a desert. The buzzing only seemed to increase the more I tried to drown it out.

"Would you shut up!" I barked as loud as I could.

As one, the cicadas stopped buzzing. I breathed a sigh of relief and laid my head down. The silence only lasted a few minutes. One by one, the cicadas started up their song again. Admitting defeat, I got to my feet and headed off toward a watering hole some distance away. I really didn't want to go out in the heat but my throat cried out for water.

As I bent down to quench my thirst, a weight pressed against my chest. Something was around my neck and no matter what I did, I could not dislodge it. Shrugging my shoulders I plunged my nose into the water. To my relief, dusk soon followed.

I don't usually eat fish but the shrinking watering holes left many floundering out in the open. Shooing off the many birds picking them off, I snatched a particularly large catfish and dragged it to dry land.

Yes, I'm aware of the irony. A catfish is the only cat I can win a fight against. After filling my belly, I stretched and laid down on the warm ground.

The rest of summer passed uneventfully. At least for the most part. Two of the young lions from the northern pride had made their way south and took over ownership of the southern pride, ousting the old male. At first, I worried they would bring their uncouth ways with them but the females were stronger than they expected and the males fell in line.

I did not see Sahara most of the summer. She usually stayed near the southern end of the territory around the lake so her absence was a bit of a mystery. What really raised my concern, however, was her brother, N'dugu. I admit that I felt grateful the unique cheetah still lived.

Near the end of summer, he spent a great deal of time in Sahara's territory, as though looking for something. Not knowing him personally, I did not approach him to discover what he sought. I only hoped it wasn't his sister.

One morning, as clouds lumbered over the horizon threatening rain, the two legs returned. They did not crest over the horizon to enter Paradise. I watch with a strange fascination as they simply stood there, overlooking my home. The pale two-legs with a mane of golden hair and fur-free face from my memory pointed in my direction. The other two, one pale and one ebon-skinned nodded and disappeared from view.

I'd seen this two-legs before. Going through all my memories, he always accompanied the other good two-legs. He was the one trying to restore Paradise. After another minute, he disappeared as well.

I watched for a long time to see if they would return. They did not but something else did. The ridge exploded with action as a pack of dogs cascaded over it. Six dogs, in fact. I jumped to my feet, wondering if I had enough time to hide. Was this it for me? Had the two-legs sealed my fate? At my advanced age, there was no way a new, younger pack would accept me.

I twisted around the trunk of a giant acacia and watched as the dogs flew down the ridge straight toward me. Something was familiar about these dogs. Just then, the wind shifted, blowing their scent into my face.

Yuri!

I ran out to greet my old pack. Somehow the two-legs had found them and brought them home. I wouldn't live out my days alone and I didn't have to rely on the hospitality of a strange pack.

They fell on me, my family, my home, once again filling me with their boundless energy. Yuri, Zephyr, Soka, Aahi, Suri, and Kal. I didn't even realize how much I had missed them. For a long time, we couldn't speak. My throat closed every time I tried to say something. Finally, when all the excitement died down, I chanced a glance back at the ridge. The pale two-legs smiled, nodded his head, and waved. Then, he disappeared once again.

"I'm so glad to be home," Yuri said, nuzzling my neck.

"What happened?" I asked. "Where have y'all been? How did you-"

"Shh," Yuri interrupted. "We will tell you all about it. But first, tell me about your adventures. Paradise seems a little different from the last time we were home and I really want to know how one little dog survived all on her own for so long."

I sighed, "It may take the rest of our lives but okay."

The others laughed as we turned and headed to the southern floodplain, our home.

"Well, just so you know, I was never alone," I began. "It all started when I became an unlikely mother to a couple of orphaned jackal pups..."

~ *fin* ~

image provided by http://www.worldwildlife.org/species/african-wild-dog

Conservation Efforts

The painted dog, or as I call them in this book, African wild dogs, aren't really dogs at all. In fact, they are more closely related to a wolf than they are to your family pet. They share similar pack mentality and familial bonds as wolves and are led by an alpha pair, which are the only dogs allowed to mate. Unlike wolves, however, the females usually leave the pack once they reach maturity to seek out a pack of their own.

Once numbering more than 500,000 and ranging throughout the greater African continent, this canid species unique to Africa is now isolated to the south and southeast. It is also one of Africa's most endangered species with around 7,000 individuals, only 1,400 of which are adults.[1] Among those are approximately 39 breeding pairs. Some recent studies suggest that there are only 3,000 dogs left in the wild. The packs are often separated by human settlements, making it difficult for new packs to form. This inbreeding avoidance can potentially lead to the species extinction within the next 100 years.[2]

The number one threat to wild dogs is humans. Whether by superstition or the belief that wild dogs threaten human lives, despite evidence to the contrary, these beautiful creatures have been hunted to near extinction.

One threat to the survival of the wild dog as a species is the zoo trade. Although all dogs in the zoo trade are supposed to be captive bred, this doesn't stop some people from skirting the law. In this book, I covered this from M'vita's perspective. Her pack, all six adults were taken by poachers, not for the intent of killing, but for the intent of breeding. It is an unfortunate reality in the zoo business for poachers to kidnap dogs from the wild, breed them in captivity, and sell their pups as captive-bred. Yuri and the rest were lucky. Most of the time, these dogs never see home again. In a documentary titled, <u>Zoo Business: The Search for the Missing Wild Dogs</u> (<u>https://www.youtube.com/watch?v=Z8OEI7u968E</u>) Journeyman Pictures uncovers this truth and the horrific conditions wild dogs are forced to live in. At the time of the film, wild dogs were not yet listed on CITES (Convention on International Trade in Endangered Species), despite their depleting wild population.

While writing *M'vita's Struggle*, I referred to many different forms of research to include documentaries, books, and conservation groups.

Solo: A Wild Dog's Tale

My greatest inspiration for the book came from the NatGeo Wild special "Solo: A Wild Dog's Tale." I used much of Solo's experience through M'vita's perspective, giving the readers insight into how a wild dog would perceive their world in those situations.

Although hyenas, wild dogs, and jackals rarely get along in the wild, I chose to highlight this unique friendship to showcase the perseverance and strong survival instincts these dogs have. M'vita, like Solo, never gave up and in the end, she overcame all the odds against her.

https://www.youtube.com/watch?v=ePgZ57SIIDI

Side-Striped Jackals

The jackals I used in this story are side-striped jackals. Unlike their cousins, the black-backed jackal, the side-stripe prefer areas of denser plant growth and have an omnivorous diet. Jackals are monogamous, like wild dogs and mate for life. While typically solitary, the young will sometimes stay with the parents way past the time they reach maturity, often helping with new litters. In most cases, wild dogs kill jackals that prove to be a nuisance.

Feeding mostly on invertebrates and small mammals, side-striped jackals will forage during certain parts of the season. In the wild, they feed exclusively on fruit when available and they have even been known to steal the feed of ducks rather than feed on the birds themselves.[3]

What's Being Done

Throughout the world, many foundations and conservation groups are coming together to raise awareness for this quickly disappearing animal. Educating local people is a great first step, as is debunking the many myths that surround them. Unfortunately, habitat fragmentation proves to be one the biggest obstacles in raising dog numbers, as well as an abundance of predators in "safe zones". One of the wild dogs' greatest threats is lions who are also isolated in certain areas of Africa.

Because of their avoidance for inbreeding, it is important that unrelated wild dogs are able to find pack mates outside of their families. Taking some dogs from a healthy area and introducing them to another is one way to ensure dog survival.

Although I did not specify which park I used in this book, I referred to Gorongosa National Park as a guide. I also used the tragic story of the park to emphasis my points. As of today, there are no wild dogs or cheetahs in the park. Their documentary, "Africa's Lost Eden" tells a tale not only of loss but also of rebirth.

Painted Dog Conservation
http://www.painteddog.org

"Create a Conservation Model that will make a lasting contribution to the future of Painted Dogs and the lives of the local people."

Painted Dog Conservation out of Zimbabwe works with the local people to help reestablish and protect wild dog populations. With over 20 years experience, it is the foundation for rehabilitating and re-introducing wild dogs to their home.

Established by Gregory Rasmussen in 1992, the foundation noted that 95% of dog mortality was caused by humans. Due to prejudice and ignorance, the dogs were at serious risk of extinction. By involving local people and educating them, they have provided a strong foundation for the dogs to rebound.

Today, they focus on four key programs: Anti-poaching units, a rehabilitation facility for injured or orphaned dogs and a way-station for transporting packs from one area to another, conservation education which includes a children's camp, visitor centre, and conservation club, and community development and outreach.

African Wild Dog Conservancy

http://www.awdconservancy.org/index.html

"Having lived and worked in the African bush for many years, we believe that investing in people and taking an adaptive grassroots approach are necessary to make wild dog conservation efforts sustainable, and indeed truly important to enable those most directly affected. The African Wild Dog Conservancy's community conservation project is in the biodiversity hotspots of northeastern and coastal Kenya, a rich mosaic of protected areas and community lands under extreme threat.

Our approach differs from a number of other projects, because we have taken the time to learn why many community-based conservation efforts have not succeeded:

•   Our project was started with the support of local people with vision, who recognize that the well-being of wildlife, plants, and people is interconnected, and that healthy ecosystems improve livelihoods.

•   Baseline information on attitudes and concerns is being collected to track project success, document and learn from mistakes, and to adapt as needed.

•   Time is being taken to build good-working relationships with local people based on trust, recognizing that there will be bumps in the road, and that conservation and development are not always compatible. We are striving to interweave traditional skills and knowledge, and cultural and religious perspectives with conservation science, training, and education."

Gorongosa National Park
http://www.gorongosa.org

"Gorongosa National Park (GNP) in Mozambique is perhaps Africa's greatest wildlife restoration story. In 2008 a 20 year Public-Private Partnership was established for the joint management of GNP between the Government of Mozambique and the Carr Foundation (Gorongosa Restoration Project), a US nonprofit organization. And on July 25th of 2016, the Government of Mozambique approved the extension of the management plan for an additional 25 years in this recent Bulletin of the Government of Mozambique.

By adopting a 21st Century conservation model of balancing the needs of wildlife and people, we are protecting and saving this beautiful wilderness, returning it to its rightful place as one of Africa's greatest parks."

What You Can Do

Each of the foundations listed in this book has numerous ways in which you can help preserve this magnificent species. Either by donating to their cause, joining their clubs or groups, or sometimes by simply signing a petition, you are helping to keep wild dogs alive.

Above all, education is the number one thing that can help to save them. Research the different links I have here or search for you own. The greatest part about technology is the abundance of information at your fingertips. Documentaries take stories like this one and bring them to life. Learn all that you can and share it with anyone who will listen. You are a guardian of nature and our wild world depends on all of us to do our part.

Additional Resources

Wildlife Conservation Society
http://www.wcs.org

"WCS is committed to protecting the world's wildlife. We have a bold vision for the future and a strategic plan to lead the way."

https://wildnet.org

"WCN's mission is to protect endangered species and preserve their natural habitats by supporting entrepreneurial conservationists who pursue innovative strategies for people and wildlife to co-exist and thrive."

World Wildlife Fund

http://www.worldwildlife.org

"Our mission is to conserve nature and reduce the most pressing threats to the diversity of life on Earth."

NATIONAL GEOGRAPHIC

http://nationalgeographic.org

"We believe in the power of science, exploration, education, and storytelling to change the world."

Resources:

1. "Lycaon pictus". IUCN Red List of Threatened Species. Retrieved 2016-10-24. http://www.iucnredlist.org/details/12436/0

2. Becker, PA; Miller, PS; Gunther, MS; Somers, MJ; Wildt, DE; Maldonado, JE (2012). "Inbreeding avoidance influences the viability of reintroduced populations of African wild dogs (Lycaon pictus)". PLoS ONE. 7 (5): e37181. https://www.ncbi.nlm.nih.gov/pmc/articles/PMC3353914/

3. IUCN SSC Canid Specialist Group. "Side-Striped Jackal". Wildlife Conservation Research Unit. Retrieved 2016-10-24 http://www.canids.org/species/view/PREKMO428071

Myaing's Endeavor
Nature's Guardians Series Book 5
(excerpt)

Chapter One: Bounty

My earliest memory comes before my eyes or ears were even open. I was surrounded by warmth, that of my mother and sister. But there was also another sensation, one that left the blind me curious. A cool dampness covered me anytime Mother would leave. This dampness filled my nose with a scent that I can only describe, even now, as life itself. My sense of smell in those earliest days allowed me to explore a world I could not see or hear and I strained against lids that wouldn't open for just a chance to see what I was missing.

Before long, I won the battle and my eyes opened to a world so green the colors blended altogether. My ears opened around the same time and the music from the forest filled my world with song. Mother smiled down at me as I took my first look at the world that I was now part of.

"Hello, little one," she said softly and licked me under the chin. Her long canines flashed for a second before disappearing and I squeaked my own hello in response.

Mother kept my sister and I hidden under heavy brush near the base of a massive tree. One of the roots towered over our heads creating a burrow-like area that not only kept us hidden but also kept us dry. Mother could just barely fit underneath it. When she left, she always reminded us to stay hidden and quiet.

Fa Ying usually listened. I, on the other hand, was a bit more adventurous. In all fairness, I didn't really start to explore our world until my legs were more steady. I could barely navigate the burrow those first few weeks. But I was born curious, always wondering about the things I could smell and hear but not see.

So, as soon as my legs would hold me without trembling, I ventured to the very edge of our shelter. A drop of water landed on my nose just as it peeked out from under the leaf cover. Surprise, I jumped back and shook my head. Being on an incline, it cause me to lose my footing and I rolled back under the protection of the root.

Fa Ying fell over, laughing so hard she wrapped her paws around her spotted belly. I rolled over and glared at her, my fur damp and sticking up at all angles. Of course, this only made her laugh more.

"Well…at least I was brave enough to try!" I scoffed, trying to regain some of my dignity.

"Myaing, Mother said to stay hidden," she answered between giggles. "Maybe you should listen."

"But it's boring just sitting around here. Don't you want to know what's out there?"

Fa Ying sighed. "Of course I do. But it will still be there when we are old enough to go out safely. You just have to be patient."

If there was one thing I wasn't, it was patient. I always pushed the limit of what I could or could not do. And I hated standing still. I looked forlornly back at the entrance. Well, if I couldn't explore the outside, I may as well entertain myself in the burrow, Fa Ying knew what was coming as soon as I smirked at her.

"Myaing, no-" she started, just before I plowed into her.

We rolled around the burrow, growling and huffing. Our tiny baby teeth were just coming in and, although they couldn't penetrated our fur, it was enough to pinch and pull. Fa Ying raked her claws over my belly, which was also ineffective and only resulted in tickling me. By the time Mother returned, we were wrapped around each other panting and giggling.

Mother stuck her head into the burrow entrance and we flashed her our brightest smile.

"Well, at least you can keep yourselves entertained while I'm gone," she said while squeezing into the tight confines of the burrow.

I loved it when Mother returned from her journeys. She brought with her smells that filled the tiny space. Each smell was like a story waiting to be told and as Fa Ying and I nursed, I imagined all the stories that went with each smell. What was that sweet smell? Did Mother traverse a land filled with honey and jasmine? What about that strong, earthy smell. She must have been exploring a deep cave.

Mother never told me what each smell was. She said, in time, I would learn for myself. Learning for myself would make the journey more magical than if she had simply told me. As my curiosity grew, I waiting impatiently for the moment when I could experience everything the world had to offer.

Also Available:

The collector set include an autographed copy of the book, a collectable plush provided by Wild Republic, and an adoption certificate. Collection can be purchased on the Nature's Guardians website: http://www.naturesguardiansbookseries.com or on https://www.amazon.com/-/e/B00FBWX9MS.

Haji's Fight for Freedom:

Follow Haji in this coming of age story about a young falcon trying to find his way in the world. Facing the death of his father at the hands of humans and then abandoned by his mother, Haji's only solace lies in the companionship of his brother, Koru. But when Koru leaves with his life-mate, Haji finds himself alone. Soon after, the same humans who killed his father, return. Find out what happens when Haji is shot from the sky!

Collector's edition includes a falcon that makes authentic bird sounds.

Timber's Gambit:

Young Timber is a grey wolf born into the largest pack in North America. Growing up as son to the great alpha, Zeus, he has the respect of the entire pack. However, after he causes a much needed hunt to fail, Zeus convince him to find a pack of his own. Facing mountain lions, rival wolf packs, and humans, Timber treks out across the wilderness in search of the companionship and protection of a pack of his own. What will Timber do when the humans come hunting for wolves?

Sahara's Plight:

Growing up on the plains of Africa is anything but easy. Sahara faces lions, starvation, and an encroaching human population. With space a valuable and limited resource, Sahara must fight tooth and nail to survive the harsh African wilderness. After a crippling lion attack, she is taken in by conservationists. Declaring her unfit to return to the wild, they send her off to a European zoo where she must learn to fit in. Unable to do so, she faces death. Fortunately, one conservationist is on her side. Together, they make a mad dash back to Africa where she is reunited with her brother, N'dugu.

M'vita's Struggle:

Having a big family means never wanting for anything. You have protection, loyalty, friendship, and affection. Most of all, you're never alone. But what happens if all of that is taken away?

M'vita was born into a large wild dog family, one of the largest ever seen. But when disaster strikes, she finds herself all alone, the sole survivor in a land of paradise without a single wild dog in sight.

Now, she has to find a way to survive and cope with her loneliness. Squaring off against predators three times her size, she comes to terms with her new role and makes unlikely allies in order to survive. After confiding her fears to an equally lost cheetah, will she finally find what she has been searching for?

Available soon:

Myaing's Endeavor:

Born into a lush tropical paradise, Myaing and his sister experience the bounty of life while under the protection of their mother. Life in the treetops is both exhilarating and frightening but for these clouded leopard cubs, it's just another day.

Unfortunately, their forest home is shrinking and their greatest predator is closing in. While their mother tries to find refuge deeper in the forest, they face other challenges, such as clashes with tigers and leopards. At every turn, she must decide if the home she chooses will be safe enough to raise her cubs.

When the time comes for the cubs to strike out on their own, Myaing chooses a path that ultimately puts him in the crosshairs. Unable to find a mate and running out of forest, he finds himself face-to-face with the very beings he has spent his entire life running from: two-legged hunters.

About the Author

Alisha M. Risen-Kent received her BA in English/Creative Writing with a minor in Graphic Design from Southern New Hampshire University in 2016, graduating with full honors. She is also a full-time writer and illustrator and a full-time mother of four (three of which are special needs). Her passions are reading, writing, drawing, photography, animals, conservation, and anything Japanese.

Passionate about animals and the future of the environment, she researches current and past events and works closely with conservation groups to ensure the information in her books is as accurate and up to date as possible.

On her down time, she participates as part of the cast at Sherwood Forest Faire where she plays Kira, the sun fae and reaches out to her readers and children that come to visit.

She currently lives in Texas with her family, her cat, and two rescued turtles.